MW00770598

I CAN'T BELIEVE I'M A DAD!

WHAT EVERY GUY MUST KNOW ABOUT PARENTING, FATHERHOOD AND HAIR LOSS

BRYAN COLLINS

BECOME A WRITER TODAY

CONTENTS

CLAIM YOUR BONUS

If you'd like a free book from Bryan or would like to read more of his work, join his newsletter at bryancollins.com

For my wife, who did more than I ever will.

PREFACE

"With great power comes great responsibility."
– Uncle Ben

I've a love/hate relationship with heroes like Peter Parker, aka Spiderman.

He's a regular nerdy New York City guy, unsure of himself and finding his way in the world. One day, while on a school field trip to a science exhibit, a radioactive spider bites him. Peter doesn't feel too good afterwards, and he goes home and falls into a deep sleep.

He awakes the next morning, feeling radically different. Peter is stronger and faster than ever before. He can talk to girls, climb walls and ceilings and fight crime. What nerdy guy wouldn't like to wake up with new self-confidence, let alone superpowers?

But the hero's journey isn't real life. Radioactive spiders don't bite regular guys, and we're unlikely to wake up one morning with superpowers.

It's the same for would-be parents. Any guy can become a parent. They only have to fertilise an egg or find a willing partner and wait around a bit. If all goes according to plan, some forty-plus weeks later, a baby arrives.

The morning after a baby's arrival, the regular guy wakes up a father on paper but may feel like he's a long way to go yet. His life will change in ways he can't imagine. He's likely to spend the first year or two mastering new skills like feeding, washing, dressing and caring for his child. Later he'll face new challenges like temper tantrums, school runs and the big talk. For eighteen years, he'll be responsible for raising another little person.

Assuming he's present, his child will shape the direction of both his and his partner's lives in unexpected and lasting ways. Along the way, he'll learn more about himself and the responsibility of raising a child than he could have imagined. He'll also encounter unusual challenges and difficult moments. The journey is long. The journey is fun. But it's not always easy.

That's what this book is about.

Becoming a dad.

I'm the kind of guy who reads an instruction manual front to back before assembling anything.

My wife complains, "You're too black and white."

I said, "I like to know where things are."

Alas, it's impossible to know where things are all the time with kids.

"Do you have them?"

"I thought you had them?"

"Well, I don't have them."

"Oh my God!"

When I'm not nerding out on instruction manuals and superhero movies, I love browsing Wikipedia, reading how-to guides and following online tutorials. I even write articles explaining how people (mostly writers) can accomplish this and that. I often wished my kids had arrived with an instruction manual, so I could assemble them. My modest kingdom for a checklist of what not to do until my kids turn eighteen.

Instead, I asked my parents, family and friends with kids for advice. I also read a lot of parenting books. With a few notable exceptions, these books are usually for or by mums. They've great parenting advice, but what about us dads when our little people pop into the world?

A few months in with baby number one, I found out the answer.

It was OK for the previous generation of dads to defer most parenting responsibilities to the child's mum, but that mindset doesn't cut it today. Nor should it. While a baby develops an unbreakable bond with their mum, they also have one with their dad. What's more, kids and teenagers need a dad and male role models in their lives too. So if you've the power over another person, you've also a responsibility to care for them.

So, some fifteen years after our firstborn unexpectedly popped into our lives, I set out to write a book based on the science of parenting. I wanted to pack it with expert interviews and research. An instruction manual the midwife or doctor should have handed me along with our son, Sam, in the delivery ward of the Rotunda hospital, back in 2006.

We now have three kids who need to be fed, entertained and placated. Having got a few chapters into writing it, I discovered I'd no interest in reading, much less writing, another dry parenting book.

Any would-be dad can find advice (much of it conflicting) from parenting experts on blogs, Instagram, YouTube, the radio, and next door. What you do with this plethora of parenting advice is a personal choice. Although, when a child gets sick or has a medical problem, best to take them to a paediatrician.

So, I threw away the third-party research and science (*well, most of it*) and mined the one thing I'm an expert in – life with *three kids*: our eldest son, Sam, who is fifteen, our daughter, Maria, who is ten, and the baby, K, who is two as of 2021.

You're probably wondering, *Why would I want to read a book about your three kids?*

Bear with me because I'm going to reveal my mistakes, so you can avoid them. When I first became a parent, these are the stories I wish an older, calmer, more experienced dad had told me quietly over a pint.

"Bryan, take a deep breath. I'll tell you what's it's really like as a dad in a growing family."

The kids had little say about which words I put into this book. Neither did a lot of the other characters in it. Anything I got right is down to my wife. For their sakes, I compressed several events, changed names, and altered additional minor biographical information. The essence of becoming a dad, at least from my point of view, remains.

The events in this book happened to me, even if my kids protest otherwise. All mistakes, with the kids or elsewhere, are my own.

AN EVERYDAY DAD'S TIMELINE

Before we begin, here's a brief history of my journey from a regular, everyday, pint-necking guy into a jeans and plaid shirt-wearing dad to three kids:

2000-2004

While employed as a care worker for people with intellectual disabilities, I train as a journalist. Friends say I ask a lot of questions. I say that's my job. I also meet my wife, Audrey.

2006

Our first son, Sam, is born (*unexpectedly*). We buy a house with a picket fence. I discover freelance journalism is harder than it looks. Newspaper editors want me to work for free. Alas, the bank doesn't agree. Hair loss commences.

2006-2007

I struggle to find regular work and dabble in full-time

parenting. Audrey pays some of the bills while working five days a week. They continue to mount up. Friends travel to Australia and send me pictures of their holidays. Hair loss progresses.

2007

An Irish recession and unemployment. Bailouts for the banks. None for struggling parents. Early quarter-life crisis.

2008

I quit journalism and return to care work. I remember how good a regular salary feels, even if it's not much. I buy a special hair-thickening shampoo. Friends return from their travels.

2009

The government insists on pay cuts for public sector workers like me. They say it's in the national interest.

2010

Our daughter, Maria, is born. I go back to college. Friends start having kids (*finally*).

2012

Marriage. I receive an offer for a dream job with a charity. It's the start of something.

2013

Turns out it's not. Dream job doesn't work out. I get fired. I return to full-time parenting for a year.

2014

A career change. I work as a copywriter for a software company and start a side business. Now, we can afford holidays in the sun. I tell everyone our family is complete. I use terms like a "gentleman's family". My wife rolls her eyes.

2018

We move house. Our second son, K, is born.

2019

Sam becomes a teenager. Early mid-life crisis ensues.

2020

I decide to write and publish a book about parenting. I discover I don't have time to write said book in a year because of parenthood.

PART ONE
THE UNEXPECTED

"I believe there's a hero in all of us, that keeps us honest, gives us strength, makes us noble, and finally allows us to die with pride. Even though sometimes we have to be steady, and give up the thing we want most. Even our dreams."

— Aunt May

ONE
D-DAY

Ten days late, first born
Fingers and toes like matchsticks.
Mother's chin, my hair.

An expectant dad is better off preparing in advance of the delivery day rather than waiting until his partner's waters break.

My girlfriend Audrey, nine months and ten days pregnant, flicked through a tattered copy of *NOW* magazine while waiting for the midwife to call her into the delivery ward.

A nurse pushed through the double doors and approached a grey-haired man sitting across the waiting room.

"Are you Tracey's father?" she said.

"I am," he said.

"Congratulations, your daughter gave birth to a healthy baby girl."

The man stood and covered his mouth, sat down, stood up and wiped his face with the back of his grizzled hand. "Can I see her?"

The nurse smiled. "Why don't you sit down, and I'll tell her you're outside?"

I wanted to buy him a cigar. I wished we were on the other side of the big day. Just then, we watched a middle-aged dad push a heavily pregnant woman, gasping and holding her belly, through the double doors.

"The other women in here are so big," said my partner.

"You're as big as they are," I said.

She frowned. "This the only time you'll ever get away with that," she said. "I wish this were over already."

Half an hour later, the midwife took us to the delivery ward, and like a long car journey, the day trundled on with the destination far from sight.

The woman in the next bed commiserated with her. "I've been here for two days!"

"Two days?! I want to be in and out tonight."

They both laughed.

The other expectant fathers sat quietly by their partners' beds or paced around the room, either too busy or worried for small talk.

An expectant dad helps their partner prepare for the birth. Depending on when and how labour starts, he drives his partner to the hospital and carries her labour and delivery bags containing a change of clothes, nappies and bags into the ward.

If you're unsure of the route or traffic, rehearse the drive in advance without the stress of your partner approaching ten centimetres dilated.

In the hospital, a dad gets drinks for his partner, asks for the midwife, knows when to hold his partner's hand and stay out the way. He bears witness to his son or daughter's arrival.

Welcome to Paris!

Every hour, when the doctor came by, Audrey asked if she was ten centimetres dilated yet – the point where the waiting stops and the pushing starts – and he'd examine her before pronouncing, "A little longer."

Audrey punctuated the waiting with walks up and down the corridor while the other expectant women shuffled past, holding their bellies, the steel handrails or their anxious partners. My role was strictly supporting. The entire day served as a reminder that would-be twenty-five-year-old dads should keep quiet in certain situations.

"Keep out of the way of the doctor but don't disappear altogether."

"No, you can't see if my waters are broken."

"Rub my back but stop fucking asking me if I'm alright."

Delivering a baby forces a woman to shed all her inhibitions with the father as a witness. The mother reveals her most intimate parts, physically and emotionally, under bright lights in front of her partner and a changing roster of nurses and doctors. She's accosted with metallic instruments, tubes, gases and injections, told not to move and when to push. It's an intense physical and emotional act that the producers of TV deliveries airbrush when glowing female leads squeeze out a sanitised baby in-between commercial breaks.

My girlfriend pushed three times to deliver Sam, but the entire labour took fourteen hours. In the end, the baby slid right out, and the nurse scooped him up and onto Audrey's chest.

"It's a boy."

I wielded the scissors to snip the umbilical cord when invited by the midwife – it was like cutting through an old wet rope.

When the midwife handed Sam to me, I wanted to say, "But, don't you know I'm not qualified? I can barely put on my pants without falling over." Instead, I mumbled, "Thanks."

You know you're a father in the same way you understand Paris is the capital of France, but climbing up the Eiffel Tower and taking it all in is a different matter. Not that we'd have time for Paris over the next few months.

The midwife cleaned up Sam and asked me to dress him. My clumsy fingers struggled with the buttons for a few minutes.

Try buttoning a babygrow before someone hands you a baby. I also recommend learning how to sterilise and prepare a bottle in advance, although the midwife handed me one from a tray. I gave Sam an ounce of warm milk while she tended to Audrey.

Each dad responds differently when they hold their son or daughter for the first time. Some new dads bond with their newborn immediately on arrival. Others turn into a documentarian and take as many selfies and pictures as they can.

I've heard horror stories of dads passing out from shock or running away to a nearby pub for celebratory drinks minutes after the baby arrives. More experienced dads slip back into a comfortable groove, drawing from a deep well of parenting experience.

For a few new dads, like me, bonding with our son took

longer than an hour or two in a postnatal ward after the adrenalin high of the preceding hours.

But he and I introduced ourselves to each other.

Dad, meet son. Son, meet dad.

Who was this stranger with a small red face and short black hair?

After bearing witness, it's a new dad's job to act as PR for their son or daughter, and announce their arrival to friends, family and the world.

People expect you to send pictures, the baby's weight, a name, whether he cried, how much milk they drank and an accurate report of mum's wellbeing.

I found all of this bewildering. The nurse or doctor handed us a baby and effectively said, "Good luck."

It was kind of like getting the keys to a Tesla Roadster. *There must be some mistake. I don't know how to drive this baby. Don't you know I'm woefully underqualified?*

Thankfully, Audrey lacked my sense of self-doubt.

We agreed on a name.

Our families were expecting news.

So, I phoned Sam's newly-minted grandparents and texted everyone else from my contacts list. I revealed how Sam didn't cry for the first hour and how his head had the human equivalent of a new car smell, depending on who was listening. They asked about my partner, and I said she's sitting up and feeding him. If they asked about me, I added, "Everything is great."

These calls and texts were my first official parenting acts, but it would be a while before I became a dad and the bond between us solidified.

Takeaways

Once your partner announces, "I'm pregnant," you might think, *My work is done*. It doesn't help that there's a lull after telling friends and family and not much to do... yet.

Surely this means more time for sitting on the couch, watching football, drinking beer and waiting until the baby arrives? Pregnancy happens to women, right?

It's only the beginning.

Your partner will need your help choosing all the baby paraphernalia and getting their room ready. That means painting, hanging shelves and minor DIY tasks. You can also prepare for the birth by attending antenatal classes, talking to other parents and asking your partner about her plans for the big day. What does she want the birth to look like, and how can you help?

Most expectant mothers describe what they want in terms of pain relief, delivering the baby in water, in hospital or at home.

After talking to friends with babies, I learnt this plan usually goes awry. Audrey wanted pain relief before Sam was born, but when the doctor came to administer an epidural, it was too late.

Your role on delivery day is primarily supporting. Once the baby arrives, people will turn to you for updates on the baby and his or her mum.

Before the baby is born, a doctor, nurse and medical team provide hands-on support at prenatal checkups and other appointments.

Afterwards, less so.

Their job is to deliver the baby safely into the world. Assuming he or she is healthy, that's as much as you can expect from the medical team.

It's a big moment for you and your partner; it's a typical day at work for them. After all, they deal with dozens of deliveries every day and lack the time or resources to check every parent knows what they're doing.

In Ireland, a public health nurse visits after six weeks to see if mother and baby are OK, but new parents are mostly left to their own devices.

When you see someone else's newborn baby, you might avoid holding them, fearing you'll drop or even hurt them accidentally.

Babies are sturdier than you think once you support their neck – although don't put that to the test! You're also highly unlikely to drop your own. Don't worry if your new role doesn't come naturally on day one or even month one.

In the 1970s, parenting expert Dr Martin Greenberg studied how new dads bond with their babies and came up with the term "engrossment".[1]

In other words, spend time caring for your newborn, and they'll absorb and preoccupy you more than any sports event or night out with friends. Get ready to take care of your baby over the next few months, and you'll gradually evolve into your new role as dad.

D-Day Tips

- Some guys want to see their child come into the world. Others worry about what a baby's arrival will look like. You're unlikely to faint, but if in doubt, hold your partner's hand and stay up the top end.
- If a friend or family member already has a newborn baby, ask if you and your partner can

spend an hour or two with them. Offer to feed or even babysit if they'll allow it. Spending time with other babies offers a real-world perspective into what lies ahead for your family. Plus, it'll alleviate any fears you have about holding a newborn.

- Strap in. Labour, especially if it's your first baby, can take a day or two. If possible, charge your phone beforehand (keep a spare charger in the car or your bag), allow for traffic, bring extra cash and your partner's overnight bag.
- Oh and figure out how the car seat works in advance. The last thing you want is to fight with the seat buckles of your car or a taxi while holding a newborn.

TWO

YEAR ONE

What's the reason for it?
That I feel such love and discontent.

———

Dads can experience postpartum depression too. We don't talk about it much.

Audrey strapped Sam into his car seat and covered him with a blue, cellular cotton blanket. I carried him from the hospital door to a waiting yellow jeep in the hospital car park.

"I've the car warmed up." His newly-commissioned grandmother tapped the heating dial.

I was twelve driving lessons into getting my licence, enough experience to get to the shops and back. Navigating rush-hour traffic with a newborn baby was a different matter.

"I'm glad you're here," I said.

"Where else would I be?" she said.

"I'll strap Sam in," said Audrey. "Quick, it's raining. Give me the seat before he gets cold."

I didn't argue. I'd no idea how all of this baby paraphernalia worked. The instruction manual was vague at best.

Audrey's mother brought the three of us back to her house, half an hour from the hospital. She'd already made up the crib in the spare room and left out a stack of nappies and baby wipes.

Audrey settled him in.

That first night, after the well-wishers had left, Sam clasped onto the baby blanket with tiny pink fingers. He didn't open his eyes much except to feed. But, every now and then, he made a faint whistling sound while breathing through his nose.

All I could think was, *How am I responsible for another human being? Thank God for his mum. She'll know what to do.*

"I love him already," my partner said.

I couldn't compete with her experiences. She'd spent nine months physically connected to the growing life inside of her, whereas I watched like a bystander at a football match.

"He's some man alright," I said.

"He needs a bottle," she said. "You're up."

I got to work.

Before Sam was born, I worried about dropping the baby or accidentally hurting him through a moment of clumsy foolishness. Listening to him suck on his milk, I knew I wouldn't drop him, but not much else.

"He looks like you, Bryan," his grandmother said one morning over tea. With a large forehead and a crinkled brow, perhaps he did. Many newborns look like their fathers. It's nature's way of encouraging new dads to stop hunting in the wild and start providing for their family.

Waiting to move into a house of our own, everything about those early weeks was fresh, like the smell of our son's head. All the time, my confidence grew through holding, changing and washing him under the supervision of Audrey and his grandmother. And when friends and family came to visit. I wanted to show them what I'd learnt. Most of our friends were childless and were curious to see how we were getting on. I would plop Sam into their laps and say, "Don't worry, babies are sturdier than you think."

One of our friends, in her mid-twenties, handed Sam straight back. "I don't want him to get sick on me."

I went out one Saturday night to the pub to wet his head and somewhat smugly told my mates, "I feel sorry for people who can't have kids." As if I'd somehow collected a lifetime's parenting experiences in a few short weeks with a newborn.

On good days, I wanted to share everything: becoming a parent was teaching me about milestones and navigating the world. On bad days, I wanted to tell my friends, "I don't have a clue what I'm doing."

When we finally moved into our own house, their generosity filled the place with balloons, baby clothes (including receipts), teddies and flowers.

The first few months with Sam at home involved many routines and rituals, and repetition built a type of quiet competency.

During a typical working week, my partner usually

went to bed early, exhausted from feeding, changing and taking care of him all day. I sterilised and prepared the following morning's bottles and then would sit up by his cot, reading.

As a dad-to-be, I'd freaked out at the prospects of changing a dirty nappy. Three months in, I thought nothing of raising Sam into the air and inhaling deeply to see if it was changing time.

During those first few months, we lived life in blocks of four hours. Feed baby, wind baby, change baby, (*try to*) put baby to sleep, comfort baby, repeat. I use the word "we" liberally here, as I broke out of this cycle each day for work.

A few months in, a friend asked if I could go out one Friday night to a big house party. I was all set. Shirt ironed. Shoes polished.

Then, Audrey announced she was meeting her friends for drinks.

"You're on daddy duty."

Her declaration was my first taste of the give and take every new parent goes through with their partner after a child is born. On a good day, it was a partnership. On a bad day, it was more like scorekeeping at a rowdy match.

"I got up early with him this morning, so that means you're up tomorrow."

"Well, I changed the last nappy, so now it's your turn."

"I cooked dinner. What you have done around here lately?"

"Worked!"

The problem with this type of scorekeeping is nobody wins, something I didn't figure out until much later.

"How are you getting on with the young lad, anyway?" my friend asked over a text message.

I took a picture of a bottle of milk next to a book and a

bottle of beer. "This parenting gig isn't so bad," I replied. But left alone with Sam, the prospect of so much responsibility stretching long into adulthood weighed on me. Despite my beer-fuelled declarations, I sometimes arrived home from work, saw the navy fold-out pram sitting in the hall and wondered, *Why do we own one of those?*

Like most new parents, I got by on broken sleep. Even if Audrey got up, I'd lie in bed listening to her feeding him and watch the clock marching towards time for work.

Ageing Five Years

It wasn't all late-night angst. Playing the role of a new dad offered a subtle rush. When I took Sam out in his buggy around the town, women stopped me in the street and said things like, "How old is he?" and "He's gorgeous, he's so small."

A few added, "You're young to be a dad."

"I know!"

I really wanted to say, *Send help fast. And can you tell me why he makes this odd sound while asleep?*

If I managed to escape at the weekend, all this responsibility made for interesting anecdotes at the bar. Friends gawked at the photos and said, "I don't know how you do it."

I enjoyed playing the novelty act within my social circle.

"There's Bryan. Did you know he has a kid now? And he's only twenty-five!"

"I know, I can't believe it either!"

As the months passed, the newborn smell faded. Sam woke up after dark, curling his legs up into his chest and howling into the night.

"What's wrong with him?" Audrey wanted to know.

But not from me. She called her mam and mined a more experienced parent for advice.

"...probably trapped wind..."

"What do I do about it, Mam?"

"...draw his legs up to his chest..."

I listened on.

Like most guys, I craved a sense of autonomy, but I was helpless and hopeless with a newborn. Who could I ask for help or advice?

After a few months, I wanted out from the middle-of-the-night feeds, early morning starts, and a routine that consumed all my free time after work and every weekend. I knew how to change a nappy, but that didn't mean I wanted to.

The same friends who'd helped me wet the baby's head left Ireland for a year in Australia, whereas I lay in bed totalling up if we'd enough to pay for a mortgage and if it was my turn to get up with the baby in the morning. *How will we pay for the next eighteen weeks, let alone the next eighteen years? Do babies really need their mothers more than their fathers and, if so, where does that leave me?*

I'd swapped the light spontaneity of my mid-twenties for responsibilities I couldn't or didn't want to carry.

I got sick of insomnia. Some nights, after Audrey went to bed and if Sam was asleep, I'd sit up to the early hours playing *Fallout* and *Call of Duty* on my Xbox 360. I drank beer, smoked joints and told myself: *Bryan, you've got this parenting gig figured out.* I got pretty good at beating four-teen-year-old Americans in *Call of Duty*, but not much else. Babies have a way of starting the day early and often before I wanted to get up.

When Audrey's maternity leave ended, I worked extra

shifts to reduce the enormous childcare costs. Some mornings, after she left for work, it took me ten to fifteen minutes to peel my groggy head off the pillow. I'd little patience or energy to feed and change Sam, get ready for work and drop him at the childminder.

I often arrived at my dead-end job stressed, late and behind. More than once, I nodded off in the bathroom in the middle of the morning.

For a while, I drank coffee all day until I couldn't stand it anymore; and it was time to swap caffeine for alcohol or video games. And repeat.

I created a nighttime routine with a hint of my old life because I couldn't accept my new one. I resented working in a job I hated to cover the cost of childcare. I was holding onto old ideas about what my life should look like. I wanted to seek out exciting risks instead of facing up to my responsibilities.

One morning at work, I was sitting on the sofa tired and a little hungover. A friendly mam in her mid-forties said to me, "Bryan, what happened?"

"What do you mean?" I said.

She pointed at my face and fell quiet.

I went to the bathroom and locked the door. Inside, I examined two large black circles around my eyes. Sam's first birthday was coming up, and I looked like I'd aged five years.

Takeaways

The first few days at home with a newborn is intoxicating, kind of like the baby's head. You've spent months waiting (and worrying) about this moment, and they're here... hungry, with wind and a dirty nappy. Friends and family want to call up and hear about the birth, see and hold the baby. They mean well, but too many visitors are overwhelming for the baby, your partner and even for you.

Remember those bars and clubs you couldn't get into because of some surly bouncer... the ones you'll have less time for now? During the first few weeks with a newborn, you can play that role at home.

"Not tonight."

"If your name isn't on the list, you're not getting in."

"Back of the line, buddy!"

After a few months, it's normal to wonder what happened to your old life, particularly if you weren't quite ready for the world of sterilisers, pacifiers and Sudocrem.

Remember, you're not alone. Your partner or the baby's mum is dealing with all of this too and recovering from pregnancy and childbirth. She's also getting a lot less sleep than you, especially if she's breastfeeding.

Ah, sleep – the elusive, golden chalice of all new parents.

It's unhelpful for mum and dad to be on duty when a newborn baby is awake during the night or suffer through prolonged crying episodes. Tag teaming and taking short breaks mean both of you can care for your infant more effectively.

Think of it like working in shifts. If you're patient and can work with your partner, the midnight feeds, early mornings and nappy runs will give way to a comfortable routine that works for everyone.

If you catch yourself pacing the halls at three a.m., covered in baby puke, bleary-eyed and wondering what's the end-game, take heart. Chances are some of your friends are finding year one with a newborn challenging too.

Tips for Surviving Year One

- Systematise as many baby tasks as possible. For example, prepare for the following day by sterilising and washing bottles in bulk instead of waiting for your baby to start crying after dark.
- New mums often descend with buggies and baby bags to each other's homes. Guys try and figure out things alone, but meeting other dads is a good way of decompressing, spending time with your newborn... and giving your partner a break.
- It's easy enough to bring a tiny baby out to a restaurant during the day as they spend a lot of time sleeping. Take advantage if possible because once they're toddlers, you'll spend most of your time running after them instead of enjoying your meal.

THREE
GUILTY

A cry rings out. Too early?
I'm up, I'm up.
Oh, you're so alive!

———

Babies and toddlers want their mums a lot, but both parents have a part to play.

"Mammy, Mammy!" [1]

I woke to the sound of shouting from his cot across the hall. Unemployed, I'd become a *de facto* full-time dad while Audrey worked five days a week. I walked into Sam's bedroom and opened the curtains.

"No Mammy today. Daddy's here!"

"Noooo!" he cried.

Aged two, Sam had a full set of teeth, blue eyes and a

receding hairline on a slightly oversized head. I thought he'd inherited hair problems from his mother's side. Years later, I discovered that my hairline was tenuous. And many kids have oversized heads.

"They grow into them," a doctor explained.

He stood up, clutched the bars of his cot and jumped up and down.

"Bop-bee!"[2]

Wearing only a pair of boxers, I went downstairs to the kitchen, rubbing bits of sleep from my eyes.

We lived in a three-bed townhouse squeezed on both sides by other houses, like bread in a slice pan. Our kitchen faced onto the street, and light poured in.

I spilt his powdered milk everywhere except into the bottle. While cleaning and swearing, the well-groomed next-door neighbour walked by our front window with her three-year-old daughter. On her way to work, no doubt.

Yes, I'm unemployed. No, I'm not dressed. And, I've no clue what I'm doing.

Five seconds of eye contact through the Venetian blinds. Five seconds of judgement. It was a lifetime.

I marched back upstairs and threw the bottle into the cot with a Thomas the Tank Engine jigsaw. This trick usually bought me about twenty minutes to lie back down in bed.

As I mentioned earlier, I spent much of 2006 and 2007 in a state of exhaustion because I stayed up late playing video games or drinking beer or smoking weed and doing anything I could to forget about the responsibility of raising a child and paying down a mortgage.

I also wanted to prove to myself and others that I was more than capable of parenting a baby without the help of his mother or more experienced parents. Conflicted was my middle name.

"Up! Up!" Sam cried with the shrillness of a military drill sergeant.

I picked him up and brought him into bed. He crawled onto my face, reaching for the glass of water on the wooden shelf overhead. The smell of a soiled, urine-filled, soggy nappy filled my nostrils.

I set him on the ground and ripped the tapes off the nappy, holding my breath. While wiping his bum, I got shit all over my fingers.

In the bathroom, I scrubbed my hands with soap and hot water. *Did my dad have this problem?*

A different generation, he deferred changing nappies to my mother whenever I dropped Sam over. The rules and expectations for dads changed years ago, and it's often disconcerting to catch glimpses of what life was like for parents of the previous generation.

My phone buzzed.

A text from Audrey: "Don't forget to put a jumper on him."

I rooted in the hot press [3] for dry clothes and turned around with a Barney the Dinosaur jumper only to find Sam swinging off the back of the stair gate.

"Oh my God, get off that quick before you fall!"

Sam grinned. "Bye, Daddy!" He let go of the stair gate, fell backwards and bounced off the steps and landed on the wooden floor with a dull thud.

They say time slows down during moments like this. They lied; it sped right up. I leapt downstairs, two steps at a time, picked Sam up and flipped him over, inspecting for injuries.

All limbs in place and pointing in the right direction. No bruises. No blood.

After a minute of crying, Sam pushed out of my arms and ran down the hall looking for his Barney book. I sat clutching a warm cup of coffee with shaking hands and watched him eat a bowl of microwaved Weetabix.

Toddlers, particularly boys, get themselves into all sorts of scrapes, tumbles and falls. It's hard work keeping them safe, but they're also sturdier than we give them credit for.

My phone buzzed again.

"How are you two getting on?"

"All fine here. Nothing to worry about. You?" I replied.

"No, Daddy!"

Sam tried to stand in his highchair. He lifted the bowl of Weetabix up in the air, and the cereal dripped down his vest and onto the floor.

"A bar!" He pointed at the kitchen shelf where we kept chocolate Smarties.

"God damn it, I'll never get this stuff out."

Scrubbing Weetabix off the kitchen floor was a particular delight the *What to Expect When You're Expecting*[4] book left out about fatherhood.

Before becoming a dad, I got up when I wanted and played video games. During my first year or two with Sam, the daily monotonous chores blindsided me. His upper lip settled into a frown. "Mammy?"

He looked around the room on the verge of tears.

"You know what, here you go."

I opened the Smarties and handed out a few. He grinned and ran off with them.

"Ta, ta!"

Becoming a dad to Sam was an exercise in guilt. I was

always battling some fresh calamity brought on by my ignorance and desires for a more comfortable life. During my
first year with him, I worried about something happening to
him on my watch.

I imagined Sam as an adult agreeing with his therapist
that his father had no business raising small kids when he
could barely look after himself. Then I'd walk in and pour a
bowl of hot Weetabix over the therapist's lap.

I also discovered mothers are far harder on themselves
than any dad. They worry about doing too much and not
enough for their baby, and that's before they go back to
work and face leaving him or her in a creche or with a
childminder.

Friends Without Kids

"You're late!" I said to Aidan.

"Traffic was a nightmare."

"You live ten minutes from here!"

Before becoming a dad, absent-minded and late friends
were amusing. Afterwards, they were irritating and self-
involved. They walked into a coffee shop or bar and said
something like, "Things were hectic. I've got so much on.
But, I'm here now."

*Like what? A small child? Do you know how long it took
me to get here, the babysitters I'd to arrange?*

I was still glad to see Aidan. A man could go mad alone
with a baby all day.

Aidan was in the middle of buying a house with his girlfriend and wanted to borrow an Xbox game.

"Stuck babysitting Sam?" he said.

"I don't think it's babysitting if he's your own."

"Say, whatever happened with his head?"

"The doctors told us not to worry."

"Are you sure?"

"You're one to talk. You've no neck!"

A compact man, Aidan had a head like a tightly-fitted screw.

When we sat down to play Xbox, Sam roared. The redness of his cheeks matched the anger in his voice. His little fingers scratched my hands when I picked him up.

After five minutes, Aidan asked, "Does he ever stop?"

"Only when his mother is here... God, I'd love a vodka."

"Those days are over, Collins."

"Easy for you to say."

Aidan once confessed to wanting four or five kids. I was envious of his freedom – he spent his days borrowing video games that his friends had no time to play. But part of me wanted Aidan to get what he deserved.[5]

I bribed Sam with a biscuit, sat him on my lap, and watched Aidan play *Call of Duty*. After eating the biscuit, he jumped down from my lap. I opened the back door for him to run out into the garden.

"Burn off some energy while you're out there!"

Violent computer games didn't interest Sam much back then. After a few minutes of running around in circles out in the garden, he returned holding a lump of grass.

"Dirty," he said.

Sam dropped the mucky, wet grass on Aidan's lap.

"Collins," said Aidan, jumping up. "I just washed this."

"Well, it's in bits," I said, laughing.

Sam, sensing he'd done something wrong, picked up a baby wipe and wiped Aidan's tracksuit bottoms.

"You better hope that's not the baby wipe I used to change his nappy," I said.

"I'm never having kids."

"You say that now. You'll see."

Operation Playground

After Sam's afternoon nap, I wanted to pass a few hours before bedtime and wear him out.

To the playground!

Buggy? Check.

Nappies? Check.

Baby wipes? Check.

Snacks? Check.

Juice? Check.

While packing up the car, beads of sweat dripped down my forehead.

Baby?

Crap. Where is he now?

Sam opened the driver's door, hopped onto the seat and banged the horn.

"What do you think you are doing?"

He grinned. "Beep, beep!"

"Come on out of there. It's time to go."[6]

He squealed with delight.

I strapped him into his car seat, turned on the radio and drove out of the estate, wondering what I'd forgotten. Leaving the house stressed me out the most since becoming a father. Before, I went where and when I wanted with little thought or planning. After, I swapped spontaneity for preparation. Leaving the house required the planning skills of a military drill sergeant.

Halfway down the road, I glanced in the rear-view mirror.

"What are you up to?"

Sam stuck two hands in the air.

Oh my God, he's out of the car seat.

"Get those arms back in before we crash."

He leaned over, his fingers centimetres from the door handle. I didn't know if the child locks worked in the banger a friend sold me on a whim.

I slammed the brakes, pulled over onto a verge and got out of the car.

"Bloody hell, this car seat!"

"Daddy?"

"Yes, yes."

I strapped Sam in, good and tight. I was terrified of letting something bad happen to Sam, due to my absent-mindedness or ignorance about how to keep him safe.

"Doddie?"[7]

Damn it!

At the playground, we threw bread at a mother duck and three ducklings swimming past. Sam took a lump of bread from my hand and stepped towards the edge of the canal.

I pulled him back quickly by the tail end of his coat.

"Ow!" he said.

"Too dangerous."

He rolled up his bottom lip."

"Come on, let's try the playground. It's safer... and I can sit down."

"Yellow," Sam said.

He pointed at a slide inside, stretching several metres into the air.

"That one's too big for you. Let's go find the baby slides."

An unshaven, blond, stocky man wearing a faded tracksuit was playing with his three kids by the baby swings and slides. We nodded at each other while Sam climbed onto the wooden seesaw with one of the boys. They bounced up and down, laughing.

Isn't it great how easily kids make friends with each other?

They bounced higher and higher, and I imagined them launching into the air and landing on the ground.

"Cillian, go easy." This man was clearly more experienced at parenting than me.

"They must keep you busy," I said.

He grunted.

The mothers in Playzone didn't have it this hard.

"How old is your lad?" the man asked.

"Two and a half," I said. "Are they all yours?"

He nodded.

"Three kids?" I said. "I can't imagine. One is more than enough."

"His mother." The man raised both his hands as if to say, what can you do?

Meanwhile, Sam climbed off the seesaw to chase a pigeon. I sat on the bench and watched him play.

Many new parents often feel guilty about what they're doing or not doing. Mothers have it harder on this front, but at the time, I'd no idea how dads could become comfortable and patient with small kids. I felt like an imposter.

Only a few years ago, I was sneaking vodka out of my parents' house and getting drunk with best friends on the street and laughing about how much we'd do once we were out of school.

While I was lost in thought, Sam ran over laughing, wrapped his arms around my leg and rested his head on my knee.

"Daddy!" he said.

I rubbed his wavy hair as if I could lodge this memory into his brain for life. I wanted to erase my everyday mistakes with ordinary experiences like the Playzone, feeding the ducks and the seesaw.

"Sam, it's time to go," I said. "Your Mam will be home soon."

"Mammy?" he said hopefully.

Then, he crunched up his red face and roared.

Takeaways

The experts say babies and toddlers need both parents. So, it's all the more perplexing for dads when they insist on "Mam. Mam. Maaaaam!" That doesn't mean you're doing a bad job. It's normal for a child to draw towards and away from you.

If you're feeling guilty about not doing enough for your son or daughter or making mistakes, that's a sign you care. Chances are your partner feels a hundred times guiltier than you about going back to work and leaving them with someone else. Like many mothers, my partner was harder on herself than I ever was.

Fun fact: When your child is older, they'll turn towards you. Until then, turn up early and often.

Peace of Mind Tips

- Invest in a quality baby car seat. Safety issues aside, it's difficult enough settling a protesting baby into a standard seat, let alone a cheap one. Ask the shop assistant to install the seat too.

And avoid leaving it down on anything except the ground, i.e. the roof of your car!

- Toddlers nap for an hour or two, up until about two years of age. It's a nice break for parents in the middle of the day. Use this time to catch up on work or, more importantly, sleep.

FOUR
PLAY

Get way up high, way down low,
And lift: you're white steel.

Happy kids like to play. Happy kids make for happy parents too.

The baby Gymboree instructor wriggled the red and yellow sock puppet in the air towards Sam's face. He scrunched up his mouth and pushed her hand away.

Usually, I dislike sock puppets too. But the instructor was in her early twenties and doing a tough job: entertaining half-a-dozen babies and toddlers in a play centre on a random Saturday morning.

When I first became a dad, I found these places noisy and stressful. I've long since made my peace with them.

Play centres are great for babies, toddlers and kids with more energy than a stressed-out dad.

When the kids are older, you can sit at a table, sipping tea or coffee, and let them play. You read or surf; they run around. Everyone's happy. While they're still babies, that's impossible as play centres mean an hour or so of lifting them up, pulling them down, following them around to generally prevent disaster.

I've spent many weekend mornings in places like these over the years. These days, I enjoy controlled environments for kids.

That Saturday morning, four mams, two dads, their kids and I went along for the ride. Sam pushed the socket puppet away, climbed over the instructor and up onto a set of monkey bars. I followed him, my hands stretched out in case of a fall.

"Don't worry, Daddy," said the instructor. She tapped the blue, orange, green, and red cushions on the floor with her toe.

"Now babies, mammies and daddies, everyone come on over," said the instructor in that overly-exaggerated voice anyone under two likes.

She guided the babies up and down the monkey bars. In between helping each child up, she produced a bottle of sanitiser from her jeggings and cleaned her hands.

"Katey is bouncing way up high, way up high, waaaay up high! Katey is bouncing way down low, way down low, waaaay down low!"

The next baby lined up, and a grizzled older dad bent over at an odd angle to pick him up.

That man needs to straighten his back and drive up with his hips.

The Gymboree was a conveyor belt of laughing, energetic kids.

"Gemma is bouncing way up high, way up high, waaaay up high! Gemma is bouncing way down low, way down low, waaaay down low!"

Ten minutes passed. Ten minutes of way up high. Waaaay down low!. When I close my eyes, I can still hear her singing.

"Now, boys and girls, let's get out the airlog."

What the hell is an airlog?

I'd never heard of this contraption before.

The instructor called the receptionist down to help, and the pair lifted an inflated white and red tube down from a large shelf at the back of the room. It was more than fifteen feet long, multicoloured and covered in a dozen small straps.

"Daddy, take Sam's hand and help him climb up with the strap, please."

More of a direction than a request, I took his hand and deadlifted him onto the airlog. He sat up on top with a big grin, kind of like a 1920s air-fighter pilot posing for a picture.

"Sam rolls way up high, way up high, way up high. Sam rolls way down low, waaaay down low, waaaay down low!!"

Once off, Sam immediately wanted to get back on and pushed past a smaller baby. The other baby frowned, on the verge of tears.

"I'm sorry about this," I said to his mam and the instructor. "Sam, let the other boys go first."

It was too late to stop him, though. He reached for the strap to pull himself back up.

"Don't worry," said the instructor. She lifted him back up. "Sam rolls way up high… come on, Daddy!"

After all the babies took turns on the airlog, the instructor rolled a large inflated ball, the size of an adult, out from a back room.

With their parents' help, the babies and toddlers climbed up onto it one by one. The instructor and mam or dad lifted them overhead and bounced each baby back down on the soft mat, laughing.

For the crescendo, the instructor produced a bubble machine. I sat on a plastic box at the back of the room while toddlers jumped in the air, clapping and bursting bubbles, and the babies crawled around laughing.

For babies and toddlers, playtime is easy. Give them a cardboard box, sit down with them for five minutes, and they're happy. Everything is new. Your every day, their entire world to experience.

After half an hour, the receptionist appeared at the back of the room with a disinfectant spray and wiped down near where I was sitting.

"Daddy, can you move up the front, please?"

I looked around, wondering who this Daddy person is.

"Daddy!" Called out the instructor from the top of the room. All the kids turned around.

That's me they're calling!

When I stood, the receptionist sprayed my spot and wiped down the equipment.

The clock struck midnight.

Pumpkin time.

"Babies, mammies and daddies. Come on over, come on over..." the instructor sang. "For shoes and stickers, shoes and stickers, shoes and stickers, aaaaaat Gym-bor-ee!"

We walked out the emergency exit, one by one, proud parents with babies in hand.

"So fun," said Sam.

"Wait, Daddy!" called out the instructor. "Don't forget your stickers."

What Kids Expect From Playtime

You wait and wait for a baby to arrive, only for them to barely respond to your presence, except when hungry or tired. Even then, their mam probably does it better. It could be the hormones. It could be the boobs. It's probably human nature.

Small babies don't play much, if at all. At best, they'll open their eyes and watch you walk across the room.

Who is this lumbering giant?

After a few months, they'll crack a smile and laugh.

I think I know that guy!

A friend sent me a picture of his newborn daughter asleep in the cot.

"She doesn't do much!" He included a puzzled emoji face.

I told him to enjoy the peace and quiet while he could.

Give babies a little time, and they'll keep you more than busy. Busy means repetition: the same songs, TV shows, stories and games on repeat. New dads need time to adjust to the way toddlers and kids like doing, watching, listening and playing the same songs, games and toys. Each phase is intense – I still have Peppa Pig flashbacks, but it doesn't last long.

Young dads like a bit of rough and tumble with their kids, particularly toddlers. Perhaps it's a dad thing. Most mams are more likely to hug and press their baby or toddler to their chest.

You can bounce toddlers on the couch, lift them in the air, throw them down on the bed, and they'll love it. All this horseplay is a great way of bonding with your kids. Kids revel in one-to-one positive time and attention from their dads.

Dads know best about when to call it quits before chasing them around the kitchen turns into crash, bang, tears, bandages and a partner who says, "I'm trying to get these kids to bed. You're not helping!"

A day minding an energetic toddler passes much more quickly and easily if they've somewhere safe and fun to burn off all their energy. Plus, they'll fall asleep much faster at nighttime.

Caution: Toddlers go and go like Duracell bunnies. Pulling the cord minutes before they go to sleep is a bad idea unless you fancy bedtime dragging on till the small hours.

Kids from about six onwards like going on adventures with dad. It's a nice little switch-up because up till this age, most children are drawn more towards their mother than their father.

You don't need to rip this dad-child adventure from the script of *Indiana Jones* either. A trip to the local hardware store to pick up lightbulbs and screws will suffice.

It's all new in their eyes.

They'll happily plod behind you in a matching plaid shirt, jeans or a dress and take extra delight if you ask them to push the trolley or carry a basket. Children love mini-jobs and keeping busy. It encourages them to feel like, "I'm in charge of things around here now, so deal with it!"

Girls also like when their dads pick them up and spin them around, put them to bed and hide behind the couch.

Watch out for signs you're lifting them too high or bouncing them too much. After all, in the land of kids, dads are giants.

Kids love spending time with their dad, telling him about their day. So it's important to take an interest in how they're feeling and ask about their hobbies and interests.

Part of the job involves setting limits for the little people in your life, so they can have some fun along the way. At least, until they find friends of their own.

Takeaways

The third-century Confucian concept *wu wei* describes effortless action. The opposite of doing, to embrace 無為 is to relax or alternate between work and rest. It describes letting go of an end goal and instead sinking into the present moment.

Small kids care little for goals. They play without looking for a result, whether it's climbing into a cardboard box, reading a book with mam or dad and bouncing on a giant, inflatable airlog.

Way up high. Way down low.

Teenagers lose some of that mindset, by swapping the cardboard box for a tablet, phone or shoes instead. Teachers emphasise exams and performance, and before you know it, welcome to the adult world of finding a job, losing a job, performance reviews and mortgages.

As adults, playing without a purpose is even harder. Instead of letting go, we distract ourselves from what matters, drowning in everyday worries.

Becoming a dad is a chance for a quiet rest.

A dad lets his kids explore and go where they go. Sometimes, dads get down on the mat and play too; on other occasions, they sit back and watch.

When they fall, hurt themselves or make a mistake, he picks them up, dusts them down and says, "Keep going!"

If somebody wants to give me a sticker for trying any of that, I'm down.

I Stood on a Block of Lego Tips

- Cleaning up Lego, blocks and jigsaws after playtime at home gets old fast. Turn it into a game they'll enjoy. Praise or reward them for a job well done. My wife taught our youngest to sing, "Everybody clean up, clean up," while putting away his Lego blocks.
- Take older children to a football match, the cinema, or even to meet one or two of your friends. They see spending the day with their dad as an escapade. The pub probably won't work, though!
- Offering your children one-on-one time also gives them time away from their "annoying" brothers or sisters.
- Children idolise other role models like superheroes, rock stars and, these days, some overpaid YouTubers. Encourage them to follow their passion but also explain online life isn't always reality.

FIVE
SICK

Cough, wheeze, splutter, cry.
Temp check. We fight over why.
Repeat. Doctor, please!

Caring for a sick child is a stressful, worrying and common experience. How a dad deals with it matters.

The rattle and wheeze of Sam's chest filled the bedroom and lit up the baby monitor.

"Not again," I pulled the pillow over my head.

"It's not his fault he's sick," said Audrey.

I looked at the alarm clock: 3.23 a.m.

That night, Sam woke up every twenty minutes crying and looking for his mam.

"I've work tomorrow," I said.

"So do I!"

Standing over his cot with a soother, Audrey opened his babygrow. "Where did this rash on his leg come from?"

"I've no idea."

We'd no family health insurance, and the local doctor on call didn't answer. My partner took Sam into the bathroom, sat him on her knee and filled the bath with warm water.

"What are you doing with him?"

I tried to take him off her. He clenched his fists, pushed into his mam and curled up in a red, angry ball.

"It'll open up his chest. My Mam used to do it."

"What's that go to do with our son?"

"Just run the hot water."

It was all but impossible to steam up our bathroom, thanks to lukewarm bathwater and a leaky window letting all the heat out.

"It's getting cold in here," I said. "He's shivering."

"We wouldn't have this problem if you'd wrapped him up properly when out today. Bring up a hot kettle," Audrey said.

"How am I going to put a kettle in the bathroom? There're no plugs in here!"

"I dunno, Bryan, get a bloody extension cord."

"That's too dangerous. A kettle in the bathroom, it could cause electrocution. I'm not doing it!"

"I'll do it myself."

"I can't deal with you right now. The baby is sick."

Audrey took him into the bed with her, and he fell asleep on her chest.

I lay awake in the spare room, wondering what was wrong with him and why I couldn't do anything about it until my alarm clock went off.

I'd returned to an old job as a care worker in a residential unit for people with intellectual disabilities. Humbled by unemployment, I vowed to turn it into a career. Plus, plugging away at freelance journalism in the middle of a recession was little better than foolish consistency. I couldn't pay the bills with an immaculate CV or a well-typed cover letter.

After a year or two of scrambling to make ends meet, I was amazed an employer was lodging money into my account regularly each week. So, I signed up for as many extra shifts as possible.

"I'm wrecked," I said at the nurse's station over my third cup of bitter instant coffee. "The baby was up all night."

An older nurse laughed.

"Get over it. How's the baby doing?"

"He had this odd rash..."

"A rash?" He stroked his white beard. "Did you try the glass test?"

"What's that?"

He explained if a baby has red or purple spots, I should press the clear side of a drinking glass against their skin.

"If the rash fades, you're OK. If the rash persists through the glass, get the baby to a hospital immediately. It could be meningitis."

"Is that serious?"

"It can be. Just ask Mike."

Mike walked into the office.

He stuck his hand in the hair and grinned.

"Hup! Hup!"

"Hup! Hup!" the nurse said before turning to me. "Read Mike's care plan later."

In his mid-thirties, Mike had orange hair, a red face and was all of sixteen stone. He spent most of his days dancing and singing to Irish country music songs by Joe Dolan, reading celebrity magazines like *Hello!* and eating as many chips and chocolate as he could get his hands on.

When Mike saw a staff member he liked, he stood up on his tippy-toes and bounced towards them, laughing, waving his hands in the air, shouting, "Hup! Hup!"

Time spent in a residential care centre[1] didn't suit Mike, though.

Over the years, he had developed several challenging behaviours. I'd have done the same if confined to a noisy unit with two dozen other men and facing a conveyor belt of underpaid staff on shift work. Mike struggled with overeating and hoarding snacks in his bedroom.

After serving dinner to the residents and writing up the daily reports, I browsed through Mike's care plan and read through a long history about his disability.

When Mike was two years old, he developed a critical and rare form of meningitis. The virus almost killed him. He recovered from meningitis, but it left him with a moderate intellectual disability. Mike's parents managed him at home for a few years, but growing older, they found his boundless energy and demands too much to contain. His care plan traced a line from catching meningitis as a child to living in full-time residential care.

"I never knew," I said to the older nurse at the end of my shift.

"And now you do. It could happen to any baby," he said. "Meningitis was even more serious in the eighties than it is now."

"I'll remember this!"

When I got home, Audrey told me Sam was teething and had a bad case of nappy rash.

"The pharmacist said it's nothing a spoonful of baby Nurofen and Caldesene powder won't fix."

The Meningitis Test

Changing nappies and cleaning up baby vomit didn't faze me as much as an errant illness. I could clean up. I could control those events. Unfortunately, that wasn't enough.

Even though we wiped down the door handles and his room with disinfectant wipes, the source of his frequent colds and flu was a mystery. They presented themselves with the regularity of unwelcome house guests after Christmas. Much later, I found out a baby or small toddler picks up every cold and bug from the creche, childminder or local play centre because their immune system isn't as well developed as adults.

One Saturday night, we were both grumbling about swapping nightclubs and bars for nappies and bottles (none of our friends had kids back then, it was a simpler time).

Before bedtime, Sam broke into a low-grade fever and wouldn't settle. Audrey examined him.

"He's got this odd rash on his leg again," she said.

"Did you perform the meningitis test?" I said.

"The what?"

I took a drinking glass from the bedside table, poured the contents down the sink and pressed it against his thigh. The red spots faded.

"It's not meningitis," I said.

"That's brilliant, Bryan, but he's still crying. Now what?"

"I've no fucking clue."

I wasn't a doctor capable of diagnosing Sam. I wasn't much of a nurse. And, on a pittance hourly wage, I wasn't even a decent provider.

The nurse from work hadn't covered what a bout of late-night tears meant. An unhappy baby is a mystery for parents to solve. A doctor, nurse or trained medical professional can help if it's serious, but parents must learn to comfort their own.

Eventually, Audrey rang her mam and talked through his symptoms. She gave him some Nurofen, and he fell asleep on her chest. If only I'd some sort of instruction manual to walk me through these moments. Instead, I was as powerless as ever.

So, while they slept upstairs, I opened up the fridge, pushed aside the bottles of milk and took out some beers. I rolled a joint and listened to Nick Cave's *No More Shall We Part*.

When I was done, I sat on the kitchen chair and plopped my head down against the cold, hard glass table.

I shook and broke into cold sweats. Fighting nausea rising from my stomach, I felt as if I were tumbling backwards faster and out of control. I stumbled off the kitchen chair, ran towards the bathroom and vomited until my eyes watered.

In my mid-twenties, having our first child was like jumping out of a plane soaring through the air at 10,000 feet.

The sheer terror of an out-of-control freefall replaced any excitement I felt about becoming a father after Sam was born. I scrambled and reached behind me, but I couldn't climb back onboard to the safety of my old life. It was like plummeting towards the ground, desperately looking for the parachute cord. The emergency cord fired in the form of hands-on support from those who knew better.

Takeaways

It's normal for kids to pick up coughs, colds and other bugs, particularly when they spend time with other kids in a childminder's or creche. I've lost count of the number of times Sam or Maria spent a few hours at the local baby gym or in a friend's house only to start coughing or sneezing the next morning.

Their immune systems aren't as well developed as adults. Kids also have an alarming habit of eating food off the floor, taking no heed of the five-second rule!

Simple things, like prompting them to wash their sticky hands early and often, help. Expect the school to get involved when they're older too. Maria's school regularly sends home directions on treating hair if there's an outbreak of head lice (oddly common in schools).

Caring for a sick child isn't always easy, but the little people in our lives are remarkably resilient. Put on a united front with your partner or their mother, even if you're worried.

When your son or daughter is sick, anyone you ask will offer an opinion about what's wrong and present a remedy. Follow your instinct and remember, Google is not your friend.

Get advice from the experts but don't treat them like a divine oracle either. One day I took Sam to the doctor, outlined his symptoms and watched the doctor type them into WebMD for a diagnosis.

Health and Wellbeing Tips

- If you're spending time with your toddler in

play centres or playgrounds, bring a pack of disinfectant wipes to clean their hands afterwards. These places are fun, but they're also a cesspit of germs and bacteria.

- Invest in a digital thermometer; it will save you a lot of second-guessing. A first aid kit is also a must unless you like dashing out in the middle of the night searching for a pharmacy.
- Keep an extra bottle of baby paracetamol or ibuprofen around the house. It's a tasty medicine toddlers love, so store it up high. My mam caught my brother and me drinking a bottle, when we were small.

SIX

DECISIONS, DECISIONS

Waiting by the window for Dad;
He's never late!

Some say deciding against kids is a little selfish, but so is deciding to have one.

An aspiring parent subconsciously decides, "I want to create another version of me!" They might be the type that offers a homeless person spare change or buys them a sandwich or coffee. Or they might plant trees to reduce their carbon footprint. But does the world need a miniature clone? And how about two or even three more?

An expectant parent is sure of what they want, though. Annoying in their happiness, they'll regale their friends and family their plans, including captive listeners who can't have or don't want kids. Some do it even if they didn't consciously decide to get pregnant in the first place.

"Kids are for the thirties!" That's what I used to declare before we'd any. As if life conforms to a twenty-something's timetable.

Over the years, most of our friends started families of their own. Some of them even overtook us. One friend and his wife had two, three and then four kids in about five years.

Pop. Pop. Pop. Pop.

"That's a lot of nappies, childminding and early starts," I said.

"I'd go again if we could afford one," he said.

Another friend had twins.

Poppity, pop, pop, pop.

(In parenting land, twins is a novelty act all of its own.)

One friend swore blind for years that he'd never have kids. He said, "It's so much work. Why would anyone put themselves through that? I don't get it."

Several years later, he announced, "I'm going to be a pappa!"

"What a turnaround," I said.

He laughed and showed me a video of them breaking the good news to his family.

A few friends had it harder: a relationship breakdown, a miscarriage, years of trying and nothing.

One friend got married several years ago and struggled to conceive. She confessed, "I'm tired of everyone asking us when we are we going to have bloody kids."

Is she any less virtuous than her friends who could have kids?

Deciding to have a child is a big decision, but it's not an achievement. That comes later. If all goes according to plan, and it might not, the nine months after conception is a mystifying, humbling miracle of nature. At least for dads. Our real work, and all of its messy mistakes, begins after the baby is born. Bonus points if the baby is born healthy and into a loving family that can provide.

Now take a deep breath. It's time to follow through with that big decision or happy accident from nine months ago. The follow-through can last a lifetime.

While employed as a care worker for people with intellectual disabilities, I met many thoughtful and loving parents who'd put in decades of work with their kids – above and beyond the call of duty.

They visited their grown-up son or daughter several times a week and took them home at Christmas and on holiday each summer. They struck me as the model of what a new parent should strive towards. Patient. Compassionate. Present.

One elderly dad, even after his wife (the primary carer) passed away, drove across town every Sunday afternoon and took his middle-aged son out for dinner in a local pub. Later, when he got sick and couldn't drive over every weekend, his son sat by the window waiting for the car to pull up outside.

"Is Dad here yet?"

When his dad felt well, he either got a taxi over or got a lift from a relative or neighbour.

Another family descended (think aunts, uncles, brothers, sisters and cousins) with magazines, CDs and treats for their son every weekend. They stayed for hours and rang the following day.

If parenting is a commitment, these parents graduated their personal masterclass with a distinction.

Some parents need more help than others, particularly those raising a child with special needs. It's hard for them today, let alone years ago when the church kept a strangle-hold over Ireland and stigmatised anyone with a child born outside wedlock or with a disability.

I worked with one resident who spent a lifetime in care and its rotating door of staff (I count myself here). His mother left him in a box at the front gates of the service when he was a baby.

I've also met some parents that showed little interest in their grown-up children.

They visited their son or daughter once or twice a year, if at all. They only ever rang the service to ask for money or complain about the standard of care.

But who am I to judge? I've no road map for what constitutes the ideal time to have a baby. Biology, consensus with partner and contraception (or lack thereof) will inter-vene on that count.

I can't offer a decision framework for a guy curious about becoming a parent beyond borrowing a family member for a day or two.

Hint: Seek permission first.

I know this much.

Not wanting a baby today doesn't mean a would-be dad will feel the same way when they hold their son or daugh-ter, or when, twelve months in, they look down at their little boy's wide-open eyes and wonder, "What did I get right to deserve you?" Nature is surprising like that.

Kids arrive with their half-formed personalities rushing in so fast it's breathtaking. Dads can set the emotional tone for their child's early life through what they say and do. Some of our personalities and mannerisms will rub off on them in surprising ways.

"Oh, he looks like you," a friend says.

"She's Daddy's girl," says another.

"He even walks like you," says a third.

Are they right or polite?

A son or daughter might walk, talk or dress like their dad and pick up some of his habits, but they're no carbon clone. The original design evolves.

When I was seven years old, my dad bought me a set of plastic aeroplanes to assemble. He liked to build them as a boy. So, I spent hours one Saturday trying to glue an F-15 fighter jet together. I wasn't dextrous, and I got glue all over my hands and on a new jumper and annoyed my mother.

Despite following the instructions, the jet broke up in my hands. My dad sat down and showed me what I was doing wrong, walking through the steps on the instructions I'd skipped.

Next, I built a model aircraft carrier without help. My dad hung it from the ceiling in my bedroom. I stopped building model aeroplanes and boats after that. I had enough of such a painstaking hobby. Much later, I figured out I just enjoyed making things, but with words, not plastic.

Perhaps that's the role of the parent, to show your kids what you enjoy. A dad lights a spark; it either takes or goes out. If all else fails, they can work it out in therapy when your stint is over.

The emerging personality of a son or daughter rubs off on dads in unexpected ways too. Sam was a surprise that reshaped the direction of our lives. Maria softened up my black-and-white view of the world. Two kids in, I learnt becoming a parent earlier than planned wasn't a novelty act after all. It is the most natural milestone in the world.

Takeaways

As a friend of other couples, it's best not to speculate too much about their situation. Some couples want everyone to share their excitement about what lies ahead. Others don't like telling people they're expecting a baby until they're a few months along. And a few might want kids but can't have them.

As a dad, you set the emotional tone for your kid's early life through your presence or absence. Caring about your family is a lifetime gig, even when they can fend for themselves.

New Arrival Tips

- When sharing the news of an imminent arrival with friends, be mindful about whether or not they want or can have kids. Not everyone will share your excitement.
- Avoid speaking in absolutes about wanting or not wanting more kids. Otherwise, people will want to know if you've changed your mind yet.

SEVEN

THE GAP

A gentleman's family:
Two kids and I'm done;
Look out! Here comes number three.

———————

A firstborn changes a guy's perspective. A second is harder and more rewarding. But things get interesting when the kids outnumber their parents.

"That's quite a gap!"

Friends, relatives and casual acquaintances used this phrase a lot after K was born. Although people offered the obligatory congratulations, they wanted to know why we'd waited eight years after Maria.

"I thought you were done," said one friend with four kids, all under ten. "You said all that stuff about a gentleman's family."

"Yeah, a boy and a girl, the full set. That's what people said to *me*."

"Now you're starting again."

"You're one to talk."

We were starting again. Parenting a baby requires a distinct set of skills compared to parenting a child or teenager, ones I hadn't practised in years.

The gap was larger than anything I'd planned and more than enough to fall into, but my wife insisted we jump, anyway. She leapt without fear or hesitation. I, on the other hand, took some time to adapt to life with a baby again.

Party Time

On Friday night, Audrey put the baby to bed and met friends for a late dinner and drinks. I'd worked a sixty-hour week and, after watching Netflix, fell into a coma sometime around ten p.m.

With baby number three, staying in didn't bother me so much. Most of our friends were all busy with kids and families of their own. A while later, I woke up from my slumber to the sound of a strange, loud noise.

The neighbours are having a bloody party.

The noise grew louder as if somebody was shouting and looking for my attention.

"Shut up!" I mumbled, squeezing the pillow against my ears.

Wait, that's not a party, that's a baby... that's our baby. We had a baby!

I sat upright in the dark and scrambled for the light switch.

"Hold on, hold on," I said.

He must be hungry. Where's the bottle? It should be here

on the bedside table. Why would someone take it? Don't they know I need it!

In a panic, I stubbed my big toe against the wooden leg of his cot.

"Ah, for fuck's sake!"

K cried even louder while I fumbled around holding my toe and looking for the bottle that I'd forgotten to bring to bed because I'd over-relied on Audrey to remember.

I ran downstairs, prepared one and spent an hour trying to settle him.

Here I am again, bumbling around in the dark, with no clue what I'm doing.

Sam was awake playing FIFA. He listened to the mini-drama and delighted in recounting it to his mother the following morning at breakfast.

"I heard Dad swearing," he said.

"You most certainly didn't!" I said.

"You should have been prepared," Audrey said. "Take the bottle up to bed next time."

"I've spent my whole life preparing."

"Obviously not."

Return to Form

Michael Phelps spent his entire life preparing for the Olympics in China and London. After winning four gold and two silver medals at London, Phelps had enough. He told the media, "I'm ready to be done. I'm ready to retire and move on to other things."

Professional athletes like Phelps sometimes take a long break because of injury, circumstances or boredom. Athletes lose their fitness and strength as their body returns to baseline. But a day will come when they return to the track, pool or weight room.

During his first retirement, Phelps travelled and kept out of the media and the pool. Two years later, he ended his retirement.

His former coach, Bob Bowman, said, "He's gotten back into good shape since September. He can give a good effort and certainly not be embarrassed. He's in enough shape to swim competitively." [1]

It so happens that Phelps's baseline far exceeds the rest of us mere mortals. That good effort translated into five gold and one silver medal in the 2016 Rio Olympics.

Phelps is an outlier in terms of his natural talents, but he still spent hours training every day for years to win gold.

Even he had to get back into the pool and face himself.

A returning athlete finds that first training session harder than anything they remember. They wonder how they will ever complete a training block, let alone post a personal best. However, they can draw from a deep well of training that altered how their brains send and receive signals to their muscles. Assuming the athlete is in good health and keeps turning up, they can regain past skills and a higher level of fitness, faster than any novice.

Raising kids isn't an Olympic sport; even though the hours during those early years feel like something ripped out from Bob Bowman's playbook, parents don't get medals for their hard work either. If you're lucky, you'll raise a somewhat well-adjusted adult who'll ring and visit.

Business writer Malcolm Gladwell popularised the idea of mastery, demanding 10,000 hours of practice. [2] Phelps put more than that in while training. At one point, he logged more than 1,800 days in a row in the pool.

Is it possible to achieve mastery as a parent? The

maths looks promising. A parent present for their son or daughter from zero to eighteen easily logs more than 10,000 hours too. But maths doesn't reveal the entire picture.

Each child comes with a unique set of wants, needs and foibles. Logging hours of experience parenting the first child doesn't necessarily carry over to the second. Go again, and you've an idea of where the road ahead leads, but plan for unexpected turns, detours and breakdowns.

That's saying nothing of how the little people in your life reinvent themselves and what they need and want every few years. From baby to child to teenager, each stage is like starting again.

If I'd understood the potential differences between each child, I'd have approached baby number two and three with a more pragmatic mindset, a willingness to admit, "I still don't know what I'm doing!"

The first few weeks with newborn number three felt like returning to the running track after rolling around on the couch, binging on pizza, beer and Netflix for months.

I believed I could slip back into an easy groove. Instead, they'd changed standard operating procedures, and I'd missed the memo.

Standard Operating Procedures

Here are a few examples of how parenting changed from one child to the next.

Exhibit A: When Sam was born, the nurses in the hospital recommended warming a bottle of milk, shaking it to remove hot spots and dabbing a drop on our wrists to check the temperature.

When K was born, the midwife was horrified at the

thought of putting a bottle in a microwave. She advised serving bottles at room temperature only.

Exhibit B: When our first child was born, he was the centre of everyone's attention. My job was to give it to him. When our third child was born, my daughter confessed one night, "I'm worried you're replacing me with the baby."

And I'm worried the three of you are replacing me!

This time around, my job is to divide attention between all three.

Audrey had far fewer problems finding her way with K. She spent Wednesday mornings at postnatal classes with a dozen new mothers and compared notes about what to do and when.

One afternoon, she arrived home from the class and explained at length how great the classes were and how much the instructor knew about babies.

"And she's running a baby massage class. I'm signing you up."

"What are you going to a baby massage class for?" I said. "Sure, we're three kids in."

"You're not listening."

"I am—"

"I said, I'm signing *you* up."

"You did what?!"

"I put your name down for the class. It's a great way of bonding with the baby."

"I already know how to bond with him."

"You might learn something."

"I might go mad."

One Saturday morning, a few weeks later, I packed up the baby and the changing bag, and I drove across town to the class.

The instructor directed me into a warm sitting room

where I met three other reluctant middle-aged dads and their babies ranging from one to six months old.

"My partner sent me here," one dad whispered.

"Mine too."

The instructor sat on a cushion on the ground in front of us. She talked about the psychology of sleeping babies for thirty minutes. I inspected her DVD collection of TV shows on the shelf.

"Now, daddies," she said, clasping her hands. "Lie baby on the ground, open the babygrow, squeeze some baby oil into your hands and warm it up."

She rubbed the palms of her hands together.

"Begin rubbing the oil into baby's legs."

I set K on a cushion and knelt beside him.

Then, I opened his white babygrow as directed, warmed up the oil and massaged it into his chubby little legs while squeezing them softly.

While we worked, the instructor explained when it was OK to rub their belly (to manage constipation or trapped wind) and when not to (if they're in discomfort).

"Daddies, it's OK to sing to baby too. In fact, I recommend it! *Humpty Dumpty sat on the wall. Humpty Dumpty had a great fall...*"

The three men beside me mumbled the lyrics, but I drew the line at Humpty Dumpty. Instead, I worked on massaging K's legs while he looked around the room at the other dads and babies.

Another baby took exception to the singing and roared until his little face turned beetroot red. His dad picked him up, apologised and took him to the kitchen for a feed and nappy change.

An hour and a half later, three mothers arrived at the door to pick up their babies and their perplexed partners. I drove home because Audrey was busy dividing up her attention with the other two kids.

"How did you find the baby massage class?" she asked when K went down for a glorious afternoon nap.

"Oh, it wasn't too bad," I said. "He seemed to enjoy it."

I put the experience to one side until a few weekends later. Audrey went to the gym one evening, around K's bedtime.

After drinking a few ounces of midwife-approved room temperate milk, K roared for his mam. He wouldn't settle despite my best efforts. Nursery rhymes still lay beyond me. So, I put my newfound skills to use.

I set him down on a changing mat and massaged his legs for a few minutes. He gazed into the distance with that vacant look babies get before they fall to sleep.

If you've ever daydreamed in class or at a big meeting only for someone to call out your name, you've had that look. And others noticed.

I rubbed his legs for a few minutes until he drifted off.

Jackpot!

I laid him down in the cot and stood over K, getting high on the gentle sound of his snores and the smell of milk, served at room temperature as per the midwife's instructions.

Like any new parent juggling multiple little people, I've learnt skills such as how to get all three out the door for a childminder, creche or school in the morning without causing World War III. Babies are challenging like that.

One Saturday, several weeks later, K was car sick on the way home from the shops. When we got home, I picked him up out of the car seat and lifted him with two hands into the house as if he were a hot coal. I stripped him in the hall, carried him upstairs and washed him down with warm water. Afterwards, he sat up on the couch eating hot toast and drinking juice.

Audrey came in from a walk and asked what happened.

"Don't worry," I said. "I've got this under control."

My plunge through the air with baby number three wasn't any less terrifying than last time around, but at least I knew where the parachute cord was and how to reach for it.

Takeaways

There's no right time to have more kids. If they're close in age, you'll spend a lot of time keeping them safe, feeding, changing and washing. But you'll also tap into economies of scale.

If there's a gap, your kids might have less in common because they're at different life stages. But an older son or daughter can help with their younger sister or brother.

If you're planning to have more kids, go in with an open mind. An approach that worked for your firstborn might not work for the new arrival.

New Arrival Tips

- Give new babies skin-to-skin contact by massaging their arms or legs for a few minutes. They respond well to it, assuming they're not hungry or tired.
- Seek instruction from parenting experts even if you're experienced with small kids. It's surprising how much practices change from one year to the next.

EIGHT
MEMBERS ONLY

Pub tunes or baby blues.
Inside meet dads old and new.
To thyself, hold true.

Most guys can become a father on paper. Becoming a dad is like joining an exclusive club and membership is for life.

I've joined many clubs over the years – cycling club, public speaking club, youth leadership club, backpacking club, athletics club, weightlifting club, book club, and even a *Star Trek* appreciation club. I stayed in some of those clubs for several years. I left other clubs after a few weeks. I've been a card-carrying member of the dad club the longest, though. Any guy can become a father. Becoming a dad is optional.

Joining the dad club isn't free, either. Here are a few expenses I've run up over the years:

- Many lazy Saturday and Sunday mornings in bed.
- Using the bathroom without answering a question through a closed door.
- Leaving the house alone and not telling anyone.
- A glorious quiff.

Ours isn't a traditional club with events, AGM and nights out at Christmas or over the holidays. Membership, once you accept, is for life.

Other Clubs

When at the office, I usually left stories from my personal life at home. I was also unsure how to ask work colleagues informal questions about office politics. Then, one day, I met Sue for lunch.

Our daughters were the same age, and they spent their evenings watching a YouTuber with pretty pink fingernails open up and assemble Kinder egg toys.

"It's amazing what our kids will watch," said Sue.

"You know she earns tens of thousands for those videos?" I said.

"We picked the wrong career!" she said.

After that, it was easy to talk to Sue about her club or ask questions about office politics or how the company worked.

Every dad needs a Sue or Dave or someone outside of their immediate family to share anecdotes with. If prompted, dads will happily regale fellow club members with war stores from their spot on the front line. And listeners take comfort knowing *my family* is *nothing like yours*.

Other club members serve as a form of social support. Aunts. Uncles. Cousins. Grandparents. Friends with kids. The neighbours.

That's what clubs are for.

In a long race, one runner gives another an energy gel, so they keep going towards the finish line without falling over. A cyclist tags a friend on Strava about an interesting bike route they can ride on Sunday morning. A group of backpackers split the hostel room bill to keep costs down. A *Star Trek* fan might even loan a friend his director's cut of the *Wrath of Khan*.

Partners

We spent two weeks a few years ago in the south of France. On the day before our flight home, Audrey and I took Maria to a pony enclosure to pass a few hours before dinner.

A white pony trotted up to the fence towards my daughter, swatting away mosquitoes with her bushy tail.

Maria said, "Look, Mam, ponies! I want to go on them. Can I?"

The instructor walked behind the pony and lifted the reins.

"I've to clean up the mobile home before we go home," said my wife.

"But I really want to go! We never see ponies at home."

"It sounds like a job for Daddy," said my wife.

I jolted upright.

Who was this mysterious "Daddy" figure my wife was describing?

It was one thing for the kids to call out, "Daddy, I need a drink," but quite another for Audrey to describe me in the third person. Even now, I still occasionally catch myself in a proverbial France, wondering, *How did we end up here?*

New Members

One warm spring evening, we sat Sam and Maria down in the sitting room for a family talk.

"Turn off the TV, put down your iPad," I said. "We have some news."

"A new baby is on the way," said my wife. "He'll be here in five months."

"Jesus Christ," said Sam, sinking into his seat. "I don't want to hear this."

"It's happening," I said, as much to myself as the rest of the room. "Get on board."

Sam rolled his eyes and put on his headphones.

"Take those off!" I said.

Maria took the announcement in more quietly and leaned against her mother. We explained when the baby would arrive, and it was a boy.

"Another boy?" said Maria. "I already live with one; they're gross."

After the conversation, my wife prepared a conciliatory hot chocolate and marshmallows for Maria while Sam decamped upstairs to play FIFA with his friends online and forget all about his parents ruining his life once again.

I leaned back on the couch.

Maria whispered, "Dad, will we still be top buddies?"

When I described wanting to protect Maria to friends, they ribbed me about a special relationship, kind of like the one between the States and the UK.

"Is she your favourite?" asked one friend.

"We don't have favourites here. Both kids are different in their own way."

"But if you had to pick..."

"Since when does that happen? This isn't a game show."

With number three on the way, that relationship faced its biggest challenge yet – a veritable Cuban Missile Crisis.

Guilt hit me with the force of a championship boxer eleven rounds in with everything to lose. Her role as the youngest supplanted by a life growing inside of her mother.

After your partner falls pregnant, she joins the club of expectant mothers. As a soon-to-be dad, you're an outsider. They get together for club meetings (baby showers) and use a language of their own, full of new terms like: trimesters, due dates and "I *can't believe* he..."

I read a few baby books when Audrey was pregnant, but it was kind of abstract. It's was like reading about life in France before landing in Paris. What's more, Audrey was already on the plane.

After the baby is born, many new dads complain their partners have no time for them anymore.

When a friend with a pregnant partner hinted at this problem, I almost suggested taking up a hobby. But free time with a newborn is a rare commodity.

"Suck it up," I said. "Babies come first."

Sure I found time to run, but we were lucky with Sam and Maria. We'd lots of family support, and our kids were healthy and manageable.

Inserting a dependent in-between two partners changes the dynamics of a relationship in unexpected ways.

Newly loved-up couples collapse into a self-contained bubble, safe from the outside world. After kids, both partners are responsible for a new life, and everything else comes second for a few years, including desires for one parent to validate the other.

Assuming a safe landing in Paris, one or both parents must dust off, drop the kids to football training or dance practice and hurry home to cook dinner.

Baby K was born five months later and very much a boy. Maria proved an enormous help and even helped name him. She fetched nappies, baby wipes and watched him while one of us showered or worked. But, like a savvy politician, she also learnt how to use the baby to get what she wanted.

"Can you put your iPad away?" I said to her one evening. "It's almost bedtime. You won't get up for school tomorrow."

Maria sighed and banged the tablet off her knees.

"The baby is the number-one person in this family," she said. "I'm tired of being in the middle. It's so unfair."

"Alright, alright. You can stay up a little while longer."

And...

"Nobody cares about me!"

"OK, OK, of course, you can have some more chocolate."

And...

"I feel like the baby gets all the attention. Nobody has time for me."

"Your Mam's arranging a play date for tomorrow, don't worry."

Maria deployed these little pleas even when the baby was in bed, asleep.

She learnt how to wade through the currents of a new family dynamic and swim with the best of them.

And the Winner Is…

I'm not the only one who gets something out of other clubs. For a few years, Maria was quieter than friends of the same age. In a room full of people, she clung to her mam's leg or hid behind mine. When an aunt or uncle visited and asked Maria questions about school, she responded in a faint voice or with a single "Yes" or "No".

Despite prompts from us to "use your big voice", Maria was shy about expressing her opinion. Then, she joined an Irish dancing troupe.

A big part of Irish dancing involves preparing for a feis or competitions in front of other dancers, parents, teachers and troupes. They practised for these competitions every Tuesday evening for two hours and sometimes on Saturday mornings.

Her teacher encouraged Maria and the rest of her troupe to rehearse at home each evening. A strict taskmistress, she rings us if Maria ever misses a class.

"You're late!"

"We're on our way…"

"Class started on the hour."

Joining a club (or, in this case, a troupe) helped Maria find an identity and confidence outside her immediate family. The trophies and medals helped too. Maria collected so many that we bought a bookshelf to hold them all.

I arrived home from work one day and found some of them in a black bag outside the house, ready for the charity shop.

That's years of practice and hard work!

"Maria, do you know some of your old trophies are outside?" I said.

"It's OK, Dad, I don't need them anymore. I don't have enough space," she said. "Anyway, I'll win more."

Her newfound confidence took her in unexpected directions. The real test came when her aunt got married.

It was a big family affair with more than 150 guests. My wife was chief bridesmaid. She wanted Maria to dance for the room after dinner. I was less sure.

What if performing in front of so many people over-whelmed her? Wasn't this the type of thing people bring up in therapy years later?

After the dinner and speeches, Maria changed into a pink and black Irish dancing costume. She stood at the top of the room, which was quiet enough to hear someone cough.

The band broke into an Irish dancing reel and Maria stepped forward. She danced solo around the room while her friends and family cheered and clapped.

Takeaways

Other dads can tell you what everyday life is like raising kids, but that's kind of like reading about an exclusive club before stepping inside.

Once a member, it's disconcerting to find life is bigger than you and your partner. Be patient. It can take months, if not a year or two, to adjust to a dad's roles and responsibilities. But, after gaining your bearings, you'll find a world of new experiences. What's more, your kids will help you see the world differently.

Kids also need a healthy way of developing their voice both inside and outside of the family unit.

Tips for Your Family AGM

- Put your kids' medals and trophies on prominent display for guests to comment on until they don't need or want them anymore.
- Enjoy dead time. As a dad, you'll spend hours dropping, collecting and waiting for your kids at practice. Bring a book, laptop or a pair of trainers.
- Unless they're older or need to know the facts of life, keep it simple when explaining a new baby is on the way.
- When a new baby arrives, announce to their big brother or sister that the baby has a present for them. It's a nice way of including everyone.

NINE

DANGER! DANGER!

How quiet our little one is, this morning.
Where is he?
What's he doing?!

Guys enjoy a sense of autonomy, but the family unit is bigger than any individual.

"Give me that!" I said.

K lifted an open bottle of dishwasher rinse aid into the air like a prize trophy, grinning, his sticky blond hair standing on end.

I stepped towards him, he stepped backwards.

It was only eleven a.m, and the kitchen counter was covered with scrambled eggs. K had also pulled all the pots and pans from the kitchen drawer, upended his box of Stick-a-Brik and topped it up with Lego Duplo.

"That's not a toy!" I said.

"No, Daddy." He drew the bottle of dishwasher liquid back.

In an effort to clean up the place before my wife arrived home from a night out in Galway, I'd plopped him down in front of TV shows. But, afflicted with a mild case of absent-mindedness, I'd left the press door under the kitchen sink open while wiping down the counters with disinfectant.

The two of us were caught in a Mexican stand-off.

I leapt and tried to snatch the bottle from K's chubby little fingers, but he ran into the sitting room, whirling the bottle around in the air, liquid flying onto the floor.

I ran. K ran faster.

I imagined him pouring the rinse aid down his throat before I could reach him and then a trip to the hospital, his stomach pumped and worse.

My Father of the Year application rescinded.

Instead of hurrying, I stopped running. He paused by the sitting-room door, unsure of where our game was leading. I took several nonchalant steps towards him like a lion sneaking up on his prey. As soon as I was within reach, I snatched the bottle from his hands.

He cried and tried to grab the bottle.

"This isn't yours."

I held the rinse aid up and read the small wet print.

"Warning: not for internal consumption. Seek medical help."

How long did he have the rinse aid?

Certainly more than a minute.

The fireplace smelt like a sterilised dishwasher, and there was a small puddle on the glass table by the couch.

A glass table! Danger everywhere.

I picked K up and smelt him. His sleeve was wet, so I

tipped him backwards to examine his mouth. I couldn't tell if chemicals were working their way down into his stomach or wafting around the sitting room from the various puddles he'd artfully created.

He looked at me with wide eyes, ready for round two.

I took him upstairs, stripped off his wet clothes, washed his mouth and observed him for a few minutes, kind of like a scientist waiting on results from a disastrous experiment.

He pushed out of my arms and snatched toothpaste from a glass on the sink.

I took his preoccupation with squeezing it onto the tiles as a sign he was OK. After the escapade with dishwasher liquid, we were both exhausted. I closed his bedroom curtains and put him down for a nap in his cot.

What if he wasn't OK? What if he'd drunk some after all?

I stepped softly across the hall, opened his bedroom door and walked in, all the while hoping the creaking floorboards wouldn't disturb him

Most parents like watching their kids, particularly babies, sleep. The gentle intake of breath, their chest rising and falling, the sucking of a soother, the two of you ensconced together in a warm cocoon. During those quiet moments, a parent can appreciate what it's like to have a child while taking a breath from the day-to-day work of raising one.

His eyes snapped open like a zombie from a horror movie.

"Daddy!"

Despite my best efforts, K kicked off his blankets and spat out his soother, and refused my directions to sleep. So, I took him down downstairs and cut up a cooked burger for his lunch.

"You're not to take bottles from the cupboard again," I said.

He stuffed another piece of burger into his mouth.

"Shows?"

What's the point of trying to explain the concept of boundaries at length to a hungry toddler with a five-second attention span? So I gave up and turned on YouTube Kids.

Safety Checks

Years one to three with a baby or toddler are a health and safety nightmare for parents. It's a wonder they survive childhood (at least, for dads like me) and reach adulthood intact. But babies and toddlers are more durable and stronger than we give them credit for. If someone watches over drunks, they must keep an eye on curious toddlers too.

Logic and reason are alien concepts in their small worlds.

When Sam was small, I patiently explained to him to wait for the green light before crossing the road. One day, when my hands were full with shopping bags, he sprinted across the street, ignoring oncoming traffic. Thankfully, the driver of the car hit the brakes in time.

It's not a sex thing either.

When Maria was the same age, I took her out for the afternoon around a local shopping centre. She started crying, so I gave her a packet of crayons to keep her busy. After a few minutes, she fell quiet. I whirled the buggy around, and she pointed to her nose. She'd stuffed a green one half an inch up her left nostril. I did my best to get it out without much luck. Finally, I bought a pair of tweezers from the pharmacist and fished out the crayon.

When I visited a friend recently, he told me about his

eight-year-old son's latest escapade: a finger jammed in a door followed by a trip to the hospital. It wasn't the first incident either. Previous highlights included a sprained ankle and a broken arm.

"He's a lot of energy," my friend said. "And he's no sense of harm."

Outside in the garden, his son was smashing a toy guitar off a rock.

Baby Seats

The day after the near-miss with K, I sealed up the wallplugs, bolted extra child locks onto the cupboards and window and checked everything worked.

Household secured.

K pointed at the white cap covering a kitchen wall socket.

"That's to stop you electrocuting yourself!" I said. "It's also for Daddy's sanity."

K could still tip over his toy box onto the kitchen floor, but the pots, cutlery and kitchen chemicals were out of reach.

He picked up on some of our new health and safety rules, though. When one of us left the stair gate open, he ran over, slammed it closed with a clang and looked up with a round expectant face.

"That gate is to stop *you* going upstairs!" I said.

The rest of the family were less enthused.

"Why do we need all these stupid locks?" said Sam.

"They're so annoying, I can't open anything," said Maria.

"They're not for you; they're for K."

"Do we need locks everywhere?" my wife asked.

"Better than a trip to A&E."

Perhaps I overdid it, but better safe than a crayon an inch deep or a half-drunk bottle of dishwasher rinse aid.

I'm all for child safety, even if paraphernalia like car and baby seats stress me out.

We spent one bank holiday weekend in Co. Waterford, on the southeast coast of Ireland. At dinner on the first night, my wife and I promised the older kids we'd take them for a cycle on Saturday morning along the Waterford Greenway.

It's about forty-six kilometres. I'd no illusions we'd ride it all –"Are we there yet?" – but an hour was more than manageable, assuming the rain held off.

The next morning was overcast but dry. We got up early for breakfast and loaded up on croissants and juice for the big cycle. The five of us met an attendant from the local bike shop in a car park at the back of the hotel.

"It'll be another twenty minutes before I have the bikes ready," said the attendant.

The baby didn't like being told he'd to wait, much less queue for a bike, so he did what babies do best: roared.

"Maybe we'll leave it?" I suggested to the older kids.

"You promised us!" Maria stamped her foot on the pavement. "This is so unfair. Just because K doesn't know how to wait."

"He's a baby," I said. "He doesn't understand waiting."

"We're going on the bikes," said my older son. "I've been looking forward to this all week."

Audrey walked the baby up and down the car park until he quietened and the bikes were ready.

"Watch him," I called after Audrey. "He's liable to hop out of that buggy."

"He's fine. He's not even two!"

After half an hour, the attendant called us, and the other waiting families and tourists, over to the bike shed. He prepped two young couples for their ride, something which drove the kids nuts.

"We were here first!" said Sam.

"I dunno, there's more of us, I guess," I said.

"It's not fair," said Maria.

"Who told you life is fair?" I said.

"Daaad!"

"Jesus Bryan, stop making things worse," said Audrey.

Finally, it was our turn.

"Guys, I'm afraid I forgot the baby seat," he said. "I'll have to go back to the shop. It's going to be at least half an hour more. I'm really sorry. This never happens."

"The baby won't wait anymore," said Audrey.

I pointed at a red basket next to the bikes.

"Surely, we can put him in there?"

"It depends on how much you like your baby," he said. "That's for dogs."

I looked at my daughter with her arms crossed, my son rolling his eyes and then at our crying baby.

"How safe is it?"

Who's In Charge Here?

Most guys I know, whether or not they'll admit it, like feeling in control. Whether it's a job, sports or a hobby.

I like to think I can control what I think about my boss, my opinion on going vegan while training for a marathon, and what I'd do with a million euros. But, it's painful to grasp onto anything external for too long. By that, I mean property, reputation and rapidly growing kids. It's understandable to want to control them, though. After all, we helped make them, so that means they're ours, right? Legal guardian. It's written in blood.

During their early lives, say up to about two, a dad's desire for control is healthy, unless he's down with the baby swigging bottles of dishwasher rinse aid, bouncing off the stairs or navigating oncoming traffic. Control cuts both ways, though. Parents gain an assortment of fears about their kids from the news, personal experience, friends and families. Some of these are irrational, but many parents ground others in fact.

I met one mother who taught her kids to wash and disinfect their hands multiple times a day. She also warned them against touching the TV remote in hotels.

"They're never cleaned properly," she said.

Another dad confessed he was afraid of what would happen when his daughter had her first alcoholic drink at a teenage party. So he took matters into his own hands and offered her one at home.

After Sam was born, Audrey insisted I learn to drive so I could take him to the childminder's and go shopping. While learning, I read news stories about car accidents, and tried to figure out the driver's crucial mistakes.

I avoided taking Sam in the car for nearly a year. Navigating roundabouts, traffic and parallel parking was stressful enough without worrying about crashing the car with him inside. I took him out in the car more out of necessity than desire.

A parent of small kids wants to keep them in eyesight, but they're going to climb out of the playpen eventually. A parent of teenagers needs to know where their son or daughter is, who they're with and what they're up to.

As a child grows, their inner life develops, and their external world widens. Teenagers push away from the orbit of their parents. A dad must decide how much gravity to exert around their growing son or daughter.

It won't happen at once, but one day, a dad discovers that they don't know all of their child's friends or how they spend large chunks of their day. Instead of walking into their child's bedroom to pick up a soother or read a bedtime story, they'll knock and ask, "Is it OK to come in?"

Grasping onto the way things were years ago is unnatural.

Until then, secure the rinse aid.

Takeaways

It's natural to take pride in your home. Having kids means ceding some of that control to the family unit.

After your son or daughter arrives, take action to keep them safe. Put child locks on the kitchen cabinets and install a stair gate. Get down on your knees and investigate the world from their eye level.

When our oldest son was two, he pulled the speaker wire from the back of an amplifier and somehow created a feedback loop of white noise. I ran downstairs to find him crying from fright. He waited until I picked him up, before vomiting all over me.

When your kids get older, you can take these minor inconveniences down. But, you'll still need to install fresh safety measures in the house that keep your kids safe, like restrictions on the home WiFi.

Don't Stick a Fork In the Plug Socket Tips

- When buying baby safety equipment online,

sort by average customer rating rather than price. Cheap safety equipment breaks quickly and easily. Is this something to skimp?

- If space permits, pick one area in your home you can call your own, like a spare bedroom or the shed. Call it your man-cave, home office or games room. It's your safe haven from the chaos of family life... and a good place for gadgets and other valuables that don't belong in small hands.

TEN
ESCAPE VALVE

Left foot, right foot fo'rd,
Beetroot red, about to burst,
Hold on love, for home.

———

*Parenting is fun, stressful and all-consuming, but new dads
can reaffirm their identity in many ways.*

"I've been thinking about death a lot more since the young
lad was born," said Michael. Although he was twelve years
older than me, we'd both became fathers for the first time
within the space of a year.

Before Sam was born, I met up with him and stayed up
late drinking and smoking weed. Afterwards, we met up
and swapped tips over tea about winding a crying baby.

"Really? I thought that was just me?" I said.

When our first son was born, I woke up in the middle of

the night, wondering when it would happen and how. I read news stories about fatal car crashes and accidental drownings.

That could be me! I remembered my life before kids and the risks I'd taken without worrying about the consequences. *It's a miracle I'm here.* And I was only twenty-six.

Michael empathised.

"Having a son gets you thinking about death a lot more. You're a long time dead, so what will you leave for them when you go?"

"But do you know what really gets me?" I said. "Death by stupidity. I can see the headline now: 'Local Balding Father Cuts Grass, Impales Himself with a Garden Rack'."

"Lovely hurling," said Michael.

That was one of Michael's euphemisms for it'll be OK. Michael is a man with many outdoor interests, including football, hurling and cutting turf.[1] I, on the other hand, hadn't quite figured out what happiness fathers could create for themselves.

All Aboard the Dad Train

A child-free young man is a captain of a solitary steam train. He hurtles along the tracks at a personally agreeable speed, with little worry. The route is his to choose, to share with friends or a partner or even travel alone.

Baby arrives, and dad spends every waking moment with them.

After becoming a dad, the train accelerates with gathering momentum towards some unknowable destination unless the driver takes care. Best to check passengers have what they need and want to do along the way. This new journey involves detours and perhaps a stop to collect more travelling companions.

Dads need a safe place or a healthy means of releasing the pressure that builds up from the responsibility and stress of driving the train – an escape valve for morbid thoughts and irrational worries to dissipate.

After a while, the family unit gains enough momentum to chug easily along the tracks on its own. Technically, a dad sits near the top of that unit, but that doesn't mean he's driving: far from it. Now and then, the train chimney releases a cloud of hot steam into the air. Otherwise, the engine will overheat and break down.

Angry passengers will disembark.

They'll send letters of complaint.

People will find their own way and not necessarily in the right direction.

I've tried a few escape valves over the years.

The pub is popular with many dads. They pass a few hours in the evening playing darts, pool or watching football and drinking with the locals or chatting to the barman.

Occasionally, after Sam was born, I tried staying out all night with friends, even if it was my turn to get up early with the baby the next day. I'd blunder through the day with a crippling hangover that was hardly worth the price of admission.

I didn't sign up for this.

I enjoyed a few drinks with friends, but I suspected the pub wouldn't work out as a hobby.

Weed and beer were a fun escape valve for a college student, perhaps, but not for a reluctant dad who must get up at six or seven a.m. to mind the baby and face the angst of depending on his partner to pay the bills.

I moped around the house for a while. But it's not

healthy or much fun to sit on the couch pondering if the roof will fall in during Sunday dinner, if I'd be electrocuted in the shower or die in a random gardening accident.

So when Michael asked me to run with a few friends from work, I said yes.

It Hurts!

I hadn't run for anything more than a bus in years. After a mile of huffing and puffing around a local housing estate, I doubled over. A stitch seared through my sides, and pains shot up my underused, spindly calves.

"I can't do it!" I said. "It's so fast."

"Walk it off, Collins," said Michael. "And then get going."

I turned up the following week, though, and I ran for a mile and a half without stopping. I turned up the week after that too. I could do that, at least.

My work friends grew bored with the sport and moved on to other pursuits, including having more kids. I joined a local athletics club, and they showed me most runners want personal bests, which means hard work. The video games, weed, and late-night morbid thoughts fell away. Over a few years, I trained for a five-kilometre race and a ten-kilometre race before moving on to longer events.

I hardly transformed myself into Usain Bolt or Eliud Kipchoge, but running for thirty minutes four or even five times a week pierced the depressive bubble I'd unknowingly wrapped myself in as a new dad.

Out on the road or the trails, the hot, sweaty tension eased quietly off me and into the cool evening air.

Sam watched me come home from a slow ten-mile run

one day and said, "Why do you run with your back slanted?"

Kids don't hold back.

I took a deep breath. "Because I've got bad form."

I knew I'd work to do. During a tough training session, an inner monologue screamed, *Stop. Pull over. Quit.*

Fear of pushing too hard. Fear of getting what you want. Fear of dying in a freak garden accident. I wanted to silence all of it.

Over the years, I took a perverse sense of pride in watching my fitness improve while my hairline receded and Sam grew. It was a measurable addictive challenge, and I was hooked.

Running instils a few disciplines any parent knows. Willingness to accept setbacks. Pausing to mark small but important achievements. The value of turning up.

Progressing involves turning up, whether for a sport, a job or the kids. You don't get a special prize for *almost* acing the big work presentation or nearly picking the kids up on time from school.

What's more, a dad doesn't quit because it's hard or they're having a bad day. Unlike runners or other athletes, dads don't retire early either. They turn up day in, day out, pausing every so often to release a little steam, so the engine keeps turning with rising momentum.

Parents want the best for their kids, even if they sometimes go about it the wrong way and must change direction.

Stack years of turning up and learning from mistakes on top of each other, and the kids will be alright. They might even thrive without a dad's help. But why take the chance?

The Replacements Are Here

"Why don't you take him with you?" said Audrey.

I looked at K, sitting on the ground, banging plastic blocks off each other with the ferocity of a miniature Einstein.

"I hope you don't mean pushing the buggy with the baby on my run? I'd pass out in this heat."

"Sam can go with you."

It was the second night of a two-week family holiday in Kos.[2]

Now fourteen, Sam was sitting by the balcony, wearing a pair of trainers, his feet propped up on the table, and thumbing through a feed on his iPhone.

"Do you want to run?" I said.

"I guess."

"Get water into you," I said. "Be quick. It's later than you think."

I picked out a route on MapMyRun that stretched along the coast road and looped back to the hotel.

Two kilometres in, I discovered the route was hillier than I'd expected. Even with the sun setting, the humidity presented unexpected challenges. A recurring niggle in my left ankle flared up, and I eased off the pace until my heart rate dropped.

"I can run faster," said Sam.

I wiped the salty sweat off my brow.

"Run ahead, son."

He ran on for a few hundred metres and then fell back.

"It's harder than I thought," he said, panting.

We got back to the apartment for cold showers and exchanged running times. Afterwards, we refuelled at the hotel buffet on Greek salad, moussaka, iced tea, and ice cream.

"How do you feel now?" I asked him.

"Good," he said. "My legs are sore, though."

"That'll happen."

The following night, I took Sam out for another ten-kilometre run along the same coast road. Beforehand, I downed a bottle of iced water.

"It's important to hydrate," I said to him. "Otherwise, one of us will pass out."

It was an even warmer evening. By kilometre seven, Sam's pace fell off again. We walked the last few hundred metres along the coast road to the hotel.

"I want to get faster," he said. "Am I eating too many carbs?"

"It's hot, much hotter than at home. I struggled too."

"I need to get fitter," he said.

"Don't we all," I said.

I could teach Sam a few skills and pass on some resources, but I couldn't offer any guarantees.

I was oddly relieved, though. I'd lost count of the number of short races I'd taken part in, only for some nippy fifteen-year-old to outpace me and almost everyone else at the last minute.

A year is long enough for a teenager to become faster and stronger and his father to become slower and heavier, but I wouldn't swap an escape valve for pining on the couch.

How to Get Overtaken by Your First Born

Sam ran sporadically after our holiday. One summer evening, he laced up his trainers and stepped outside while I put the baby to bed.

He returned home an hour later, his t-shirt soaked, listening to music on his AirPods. While I cooked pasta, he prepared a pot of lumpy mashed potatoes.

"How far did you run?" I said.

Silence.

"Hello?" I waved.

Sam removed his AirPods.

"What?"

"Your run?"

"Oh, about ten kilometres."

"How long did that take you?"

"I ran around the college in about forty-seven minutes."

"Forty-seven minutes?!"

He grinned.

"Am I fast?"

My personal best for a ten-kilometre was forty-five minutes, and my normal time averaged around fifty. I'm hardly a fast runner, but I've spent enough time and money on the sport to hope I can run faster than those who rarely train. Sam was reasonably fit, although he preferred playing sports like hurling rather than putting in miles on the road or at a running track.

"Show me your time," I said, like a detective demanding proof or an alibi.

Sam produced his iPhone, opened up the running app, and produced his splits.

The numbers didn't lie. He ran ten kilometres in about forty-eight minutes thirty seconds, which was worryingly close to my average pace. And his heart rate was gloriously low, suggesting an inbuilt natural fitness that I lack.

"Was that good?" he said.

Surely his Apple Watch isn't as accurate as my Garmin running watch!

"Your potatoes are burning."

After dinner, I spent half an hour Googling "teenager run times vs adult run times". The results weren't good. I could only expect his times to improve, even if he didn't put in much more effort, while mine would gradually decline.

It's galling to think you're a young guy and then suddenly find yourself lining up with the other older dads on the start line. The painful truth is he will become faster and stronger than I am. We play the game for as long as possible without knowing how it will end. We play until it's someone else's turn.

I took Sam out for an easy run along the local canal bank one evening. It was overcast and cloudy, not too hot or cold. We didn't need hats or running gloves, and dehydration was hardly an issue. My ankle ached, and I considered abandoning the run, but Sam was only metres behind.

A few miles in, with blood pumping and my legs and lungs working hard, I felt more alive than I had in days. Although the sport doesn't offer any guarantees, I could still choose to play, step out, put one foot in front of the other and keep going.

"Try and keep up," I called out.

I picked up the pace, listening to the steady churn of Sam's feet on the gravel a few metres behind me. His relaxed breathing suggested *I've got this too.*

The Royal Canal stretched east and west of Maynooth. A brilliant, shimmering orange sun pierced through the parting grey clouds. My watch marked the passing milestones with a beep, but we'd a bit to go yet. I'd trained for this run. I could keep going for miles.

Unless my son catches me first.

Takeaways

Life with small kids can feel like being swallowed whole. They need a lot of attention from both parents and sometimes more than we can give without recharging. Figuring out how to raise and care for your firstborn and negotiate parenting with your partner isn't easy.

New dads carry baggage from childhood and family experiences into their new roles. What's more, you may still be figuring out what direction you want your life, career and relationships to take.

Becoming a young dad doesn't mean forgetting your goals and plans for the future. If anything, it will clarify what's important versus a waste of time.

It's also a good time to finally work on and resolve past issues.

Self-care becomes all the more important with small kids unless you fancy burning out and snapping at them. So, agree with your partner on who's minding the baby and when. Aim for an equal division of labour. Think back to your plans pre-parenting and pre-career.

What activities did you enjoy? Did someone show you the way, or did you learn from friends? Pick a healthy interest or pursuit to cultivate outside of family life.

Some guys like burying themselves in work, but that presents its own problems if a job doesn't work out or you change career. Plus, working eighty-hour weeks is a surefire recipe for domestic strife.

It's difficult to find free time during the early years with a small child. You might only get an hour or two each week for a hobby. But that's often enough. You'll gradually earn more time back, especially when they start school.

Plus, as your child grows older, side-interests could give you and your son or daughter something new to bond over.

Chances are, they could benefit from some instruction too. Even if you don't share the same interests, can you find someone who can teach them the basics via a class or coaching?

Self-care Tips

- A good escape valve leaves you with more time and energy for the kids when you return... rather than emptying you out, like that hollow feeling of a boozy night out or hours whiled away on Facebook. I picked running, but another dad I know enjoys fishing. Yours might be brewing beer, cycling or martial arts. The key is to do something you enjoy that offers a release from life as a dad and work.
- You're not the only one who needs an escape valve. If your partner gets time to see her friends or live a little outside of the home, everyone wins.

PART TWO
BECOMING A DAD

"No man can win every battle, but no man should
fall without a struggle."
   – Peter Parker

ELEVEN

THE PROVIDER

She's bursting bubbles.
And growing tall.
Beneath the moonlight.

―――――――――

A young dad faces a dilemma: become a stay-at-home parent or provide. Choose wisely.

New young dads face two career choices. Stay at home and raise a son or daughter full-time for a few years; or work, and work hard.

The first option is a fine way to spend time with them while they're small. It's also an odd combination of rewarding and isolating. Stay-at-home parents witness their kids grow up, but they don't get Christmas parties, bonuses, promotions or much acknowledgement for a job well done.

This choice also assumes your partner is working or

you've a means of paying the bills. The second option means doubling down on a career. Before a baby arrives, it's fine to try on different jobs and drift from one to the next until you find one you love... or can at least get out of bed for.

Nappies, baby milk and childminders or creches aren't cheap. Somebody needs to bring home a reliable salary for the family. As a working parent, that means YOU. For most working dads, a job is an important part of how they spend the day. It's good to bring something home for the family, even if a wife or partner earns too.

Perhaps this instinct goes back to when we lived in caves and marched out into the wild in packs, clubbing animals and dragging them home for everyone to eat. Unfortunately, it's not so simple in the twenty-first century, and the start of any young guy's career is tricky enough at the best of times.

When Sam was small, I tried making it as a journalist. I spent weeks emailing out CVs and cover letters to every newspaper with no response.

I pressed one responsive editor for more answers.

"I can work," I said. "I only need a chance."

"The newspaper is making cutbacks," he said. "With the recession, it's not a good time for hiring."

"What about freelance gigs? How can I land more of those?"

"Ring the news editor, send them your CV and some article ideas and then follow it up."

But articles about what? I didn't know where to start.

My persistence almost paid off.

The editor of a magazine, a two-and-a-half-hour train and bus commute away from home, invited me to work for free for a few weeks.

Even if I could figure out how to pay for childminding while working for free, I resented the invitation. I didn't spend four years in college to hawk myself for nothing. *Don't they know I have a degree?* I wanted a linear, upward career path. Work hard at job A, get offered jobs B and C. Work hard at job C and field offers for jobs D, E and F. Editor of a national newspaper by forty? Certainly.

I wasted my education figuring out how to meet women and get drunk or high on the cheap instead of planning for work post-graduation, to say nothing of learning how to raise and support a family. I also never considered the state of the job market in Ireland. With only a few big media organisations in the country, it was like swimming in a small lake.

Hundreds of graduates dived in every year armed with degrees, contacts and high hopes. Meanwhile, larger, more experienced sharks circled, waiting to feed. But food was in short supply.

Our small family, stuck on a leaky boat, struggled to pay the bills on time and survive from payday to payday – and that was on a good month. The recession was a financial tsunami that drove many friends from the country. Our prospects looked grim.

One weekend, I gathered up all the coppers and silver coins from the house, put them in a black bag and fed a spare change machine at Tesco's supermarket.

While waiting for the machine to tally up, I picked up a copy of *The Irish Times*. Working at that newspaper represented my dream job and one painfully out of reach. The headline read, "Jobless rate at the highest level in four years".

Inside, sandwiched between articles about bank bailouts and austerity measures, I read a feature questioning

if degrees from a few years ago were already out of date...
like my journalism degree from 2004.

Ding. Ding-Ding.

€82.17.

And that was after Tesco's five per cent cut. Not bad for
an hour's work rooting through the drawers, back of the
couch and the spare change jar.

I bought a packet of nappies, baby wipes, chocolate and
beer with the spare change.

My partner had a full-time job, so we could still afford
our mortgage. But money was tight. And small kids are
always in need of more food, clothes, shoes and toys.

Most dads put themselves under pressure to provide;
struggling to make ends meet is a demoralising experience.

Hunting for spare change around the house and
depending on my partner's salary wasn't what I had in mind
when I set out to become a journalist.

Late at night, I watched current affairs shows like *Prime
Time* on RTE.[1]

I couldn't believe the government was bailing out big
businesses and banks. They left new families and struggling
parents to figure out how to survive and justified it with
clichés like "in the national interest".

One chairman of a bailed-out Irish bank even told the
government to cut "the sacred cows of Irish society" – children, the elderly and healthcare.

Lying in bed late at night, I worried if I didn't find reliable work soon, the endeavour would capsize and take us
with it.

The 168-hour Work Week

One Saturday morning, we cleaned out the attic and donated some of Sam's older clothes to the charity shop. I loaded up my old car with rubbish and drove to the city dump twenty minutes away, off the M50.

On a whim, I took my old newspaper cuttings from the various newspapers which had reluctantly published my work over the years.

The dump smelt like rotten eggs and sour milk. I emptied out the rubbish into a recycling landfill. When I opened the cardboard box of newspaper cuttings, a gust of wind scattered the newspapers across the dump. I spent ten minutes picking sodden yellow newspapers off the ground, wet ink from my byline running down my hands.

It took a combination of luck, patience and a return to college to reboot my career. After a few years, I found work with a British software company as a junior copywriter.

On the Sunday evening before my career reboot, we visited my mother-in-law with Maria and Sam.

"Someone has a dirty nappy," said my mother-in-law.

Maria, aged two, held up her hands as if to say, "Don't look at me!"

"Who do you want to change your nappy?" she said to Maria, looking first at Audrey and then at me.

A *Matrix* moment.

Usually, babies opt for the blue pill. They put their mothers first. During the first few years with Sam, I resented the way he called "Maaam" all the time and pushed me away. Later on, I found it endearing.

It's basic biology. After all, a mother spends nine months growing the baby inside of her. Why would any dad want to compete with that?

But this time, Maria ran into my arms, buried her head in my lap and opted for the red pill.

After I changed Maria, my mother-in-law said: "I know you wouldn't have chosen this, Bryan, but isn't it great that you got to spend so much time with Maria over the past year?"

After months of long days at the office, I secured a permanent job, one with a manager and people I liked, but recession, rejection and unemployment had left their mark.

I vowed to never become so dependent on one career or a single employer again. Providing for a family means having a backup plan for when things go awry.

The salary bump was nice, but I got up at between five and six each morning to write on the side. I'd also started a website about the craft of writing that gradually, and somewhat unexpectedly, grew into an online business.

I balanced my job as a copywriter with the new online business, writing and the kids. I transitioned from having more free time than I knew what to do with to almost none.

While unemployed, I put the kids first, albeit not always intentionally. A new job meant putting my career first by staying late in the office or taking courses at night.

Putting friendships first, through late nights out or trips away with the lads, meant spending less time at home, taking work courses or writing.

I never found a happy equilibrium. Instead, I approached a job and side business, family, friendships and even writing as like dials on a hob. Turning up one meant taking fuel away from the other, but sometimes you gotta sizzle that steak.

After a big company quarterly review, I went out with the team for a few beers in an overpriced Dublin restaurant.

"You're very focused," a work friend said over chicken

wings. "I'm pretending to work on Friday afternoon, and there you are, still going."

"Hah! Audrey says I'm obsessed, that I should relax more."

"She might be right," he said.

"The thing is, I worry they're going to find out I don't know what I'm doing and fire me."

He laughed.

"I thought I was the only person who worried about that."

"Don't be ridiculous," I said. "You're good at your job. Anyone can see it."

"Thanks."

I sipped my beer. "If this were the real world, we'd be mates."

"Bryan," he said. "We are."

My personal life took a back seat, and I turned up the heat on work. I took every online course I could afford and earned a few promotions. Obsession. Focus. Two sides of the same coin.

Sizzle. Sizzle.

Finally, I built up some financial protection for a future recession. I also gained skills to survive in the next job and the one after that. I played the long game. I wanted to play for the next eighteen years. A good chunk of life is friends, family and work, and not always in that order.

I'll get you to college, son, I swear.

Meanwhile, Sam and Maria grew older, and we didn't have to spend as much on childminding and afterschool care. It helped that friends were gradually having kids and dealing with their particular juggling acts.

Having kids. Having more kids. Competing family

dynamics. Complaining about the cost of childcare and a mortgage.

Been there, done that.

I met one overworked friend at Christmas, who was head of legal for a US corporate.

He told me, "I fall asleep some nights in the office on a bread roll. I wake up at two, face down on my keyboard, and pick cheese out of my beard."

"That doesn't sound much fun."

"How much do you work, Bryan?"

I took a deep breath.

"Every day," I said.

Working hard paid off, to a point. One year, my corporate employer paid me a generous Christmas bonus. It was more than I expected.

"Thanks for all your hard work this fiscal year," said my old boss.

"I'm looking forward to a strong quarter," I said.

Ah, fiscals. Quarters. Kick-offs. Annual reviews. I was game with corporate speak.

I promptly used the extra cash to book a trip to Disney World in Florida. A reward for a job well done.

On the first evening, we got lost in the Magic Kingdom. Audrey sat on a small wall along the town square, searching a foldout map for the car park.

Sam sat beside her on his phone.

"The car park is that way, Mam."

"If your Dad could remember where we parked."

A machine at a nearby souvenir shop blew bubbles in the air, its kaleidoscope transforming them into glorious greens, yellows, reds and blues.

The bubbles rose slowly over the square and into the warm night sky, while Maria, four fiscals in, jumped from one foot to the other, clapping and bursting as many as she could reach.

Takeaways

Becoming a young dad often means starting a career and juggling childcare costs with running a home and raising a family. If you're frustrated about falling behind peers, particularly those without kids, fear not. The first few years of raising a son or daughter are the most financially draining, even if your partner works too. Providing gets easier. You'll probably earn more and costs will come down.

It doesn't happen overnight, but becoming a dad helps many guys gain a better work-life balance and spend their free time more meaningfully.

Consider how you spent the past few weeks or months. What strikes you as time well-spent versus time wasted? Are you moving towards or away from what you and your family want?

Family, work and friendships are important, but will you accept a compromise in one area to focus on another, if only for a year or two? For example, your partner may support you going to college to advance a career. Or vice versa.

Weed out anything that doesn't align with your family's core values. Whatever your choice, remember a career can be rewarding, but for a few short years, you're their entire world. That's a bigger reward than any regular job can offer.

Tips for Stressed-out Providers

- Set clear goals for what your ideal career looks

like, and not only in terms of money and status. What will your ideal work-family life balance look like?

- Small kids wonder where Dad goes all day. Explain it to them. Better yet, bring them in for the day if it's company culture.
- If you're spending more than a few weeks as a stay-at-home parent, allocate a few hours each week for online learning or a side-gig. The kids will get older, and you'll face the workplace at some point unless you win the Lotto!

TWELVE

GIRLS AND BOYS

He's pushing a pink buggy.
She crashing a monster truck.
We're smashing conventions.

———

Dads bring unconscious bias to their perception of girls and boys. The question is, how many of these biases are true?

"I'm so excited!" said Maria, aged seven. "Will I get a present?"

"Were you good this year?" I said.

"I think so," she said. "I hope it's a Disney princess."

We were driving across town to see Santa, in an arboretum of all places.

Santa charges extra for visits outside run-of-the-mill shopping centres, and my wife had booked months in advance.

Our visit to see Santa started out on a pleasant note. We got into a miniature train and travelled around the gardens outside the arboretum admiring the sparkling lights, listening to Christmas songs and drinking hot chocolate. Afterwards, we marched into a stately room with an open fire and queued to see Santa. Maria climbed up onto his lap while Audrey took a picture with her smartphone.

"And what would you like for the big day?" said Santa.

"A Disney princess," she whispered.

"Have you been a good girl this year?"

"I think so," she said.

"Well, I'll check my list."

Maria looked at her mother for the green light.

"Let's see what we have here," said Santa.

The elf beside Santa produced a large box wrapped with a yellow bow.

"Wow!" Maria said, tugging on the bow. "Thanks, Santa."

She hopped down off his lap and took the box over to us. But when she opened it, Maria's eyes narrowed.

"What is it?" she asked me.

I shook the box and examined the front of it.

Kids Garden Starter Kit. Includes Rake.

"You need to go over and say something," said my wife.

"She might use it..."

"She'll never use it."

I walked back to the elf and coughed to get her attention.

"Excuse me," I whispered, in case other parents took exception to my imminent confrontation with the elf. "The thing is, it's the middle of winter and..."

"Yes?"

"Maria doesn't really like... is there anything more suitable for a girl her age?"

"For A GIRL?"

The elf arched her green eyebrows forty-five degrees. The waves of disapproval emanated from every fibre.

"We don't give one type of present for boys and another type for girls," said the elf. "We offer gender-neutral presents that *all the kids can enjoy*."

A line of parents and kids wrapped in winter coats and scarves were queuing up to collect their gardening kits from Santa.

"What's taking so long, Dad?" said one little boy.

Her mother tapped her foot.

The elf rolled her eyes.

"Is there anything else she can get?"

"We have presents all the kids can enjoy!"

Yikes!

I was about to go viral on Twitter for all the wrong reasons.

"We'll leave it so, thanks anyway," I said.

I trudged back to Maria.

"I've done the best I can," I said. "You might use it in the spring."

"The spring? That's ages away."

Was I guilty of conforming to a gender stereotype? Certainly, but Maria enjoyed pink and purple glittery gifts, princess castles and even songs from Disney princess films. As somebody who likes to write, I spend lots of time rooting out clichés, but you can find truth in a few if you know where to look.

Still, I couldn't help but wonder if the differences between boys and girls are more down to nature or nurture?

Did Maria like princess castles and my older son weight-lifting because of their parents, or biology?

It's a Girl... No, No, Wait!

When Audrey was pregnant with Sam, people asked us, "Are you finding out the sex?"

After checking with Audrey, I told them: "Of course, the whole thing is enough of a surprise."

"Boys will wreck your house," said an older friend, more experienced in the mysterious ways of parenting. "Girls will wreck your head."

"I'm sure it's a girl," said Audrey.

Several months later, we went into the Rotunda hospital for the big twenty-four week scan.

"It looks like a girl," said the nurse. "No, no, wait. Congratulations. You're having a boy!"

I searched a grainy print-out for evidence of a small penis, my son and heir.

Audrey didn't question it.

She bought blue babygrows. Still in shock, I bought beer and cans of blue paint. It was 2006. It was a different time.

A few years later, when Audrey became pregnant again, she convinced herself it was a girl.

At the big scan, the nurse announced, "Congratulations. You're having a girl!"

In the months leading up to Maria's birth, we embraced every cliché and stereotype. I painted her bedroom walls a dark and light shade of pink. Audrey hung pink curtains and bought pink sheets, babygrows and blankets.

Her delivery stretched from eight that morning till after midnight. She arrived quietly, a scrunched up ball of red and pink.

Audrey wrapped her up in baby blankets.

All that pink was blinding.

After she arrived, I said to friends, "I wish girls came with an instruction manual."

With help from Audrey, her aunts and grandmothers, I slowly found my way.

A few years later, Maria told me. "You know, I don't even like pink. Purple is my favourite colour."

A few years later, pregnant for a third time, Audrey insisted she was having yet another girl.

"Congratulations," said the nurse. "It's a boy!"

I didn't bother with the cans of blue or pink paint or other gender stereotypes this time around and opted for eggshell-white bedroom walls. Today, K plays with cars, trucks and likes smashing fresh eggs on the ground. He also enjoys pushing a pink buggy with his baby around the estate.

Perhaps I'm conscious of setting gender stereotypes too early. Perhaps I'm afraid of woke elves. Or perhaps I'm lazy.

Testosterone Up

Audrey was right. She really was having girls each time, at least at first.

All babies start life as females.

If the Y chromosome activates around the eight-week mark, the baby grows testicles and a penis and undergoes other physical changes in the womb.

He was once she.[1,2]

After birth, a baby boy's body contains the same level of testosterone as a twelve-year-old. His dad experiences a drop-off in testosterone production and a rise in vasopressin, a bonding hormone.

A boy has more energy than some girls, picking things up off the floor, eating them and seeing what he can flush down the toilet.

He climbs on chairs, smashes eggs on the floor and runs around the house.

In our family, my sister-in-law gave birth to a baby girl three and a half months after our third son was born. It didn't take long for the age gap to close. She talked, counted, sung and called out colours first, despite our son's three-and-a-half-month advantage. On the other hand, K took delight in walking, running and climbing up on chairs, stairs and over anyone sitting beside him.

Testosterone levels in a small boy level off during the first few years, but dads, don't settle down on the couch for too long. Sometime around four, a boy's testosterone production levels double. At this age, they're still developing their gross muscle wiring too. This testosterone translates into more playful energy, but it can erupt into temper tantrums and other odd episodes.

I'll never forget when Sam, aged four, kicked the dishwasher door, and, red in the face, told us, "I won't eat my dinner!"

He also enjoyed stripping off naked and running around the house. We barely managed to keep a lid on his extra energy. Sending him to football training (with his clothes on) helped.

For a while, he became, as one grandparent said, "A real handful."

Maria never kicked the dishwasher or ran around the house naked. Instead, she deployed subtler weapons like:

"Nobody in this family cares about me!"

And:

"You're ruining my life."

Boys need more help than girls thinking actions through and understanding their emotions. When they turn thirteen, they also go through a dopey stage.

My wife and I spent a year or so dropping forgotten lunchboxes, hurls, jumpers and coats to Sam in school, at his friend's house and at football training.

One Monday afternoon, he texted me.

"I forgot my bag for PE. Can you drop it up?"

Although we live near his school, I was mired in a work project gone awry, and I said no.

At dinner, he complained, "Dad wouldn't drop up my PE gear."

"No more," I said to Audrey. "He has to learn sometime!"

I felt guilty about leaving him to his own devices until a school meeting for teachers and parents.

"They're teenagers now. Parents, let them make their own mistakes," said the year head.

You're talking my language, sir!

Around fourteen, a teenage boy's testosterone levels increase by up to 800 per cent compared to toddlerhood. All aboard! The train to adulthood is about to leave the station.

Girls at the same age, on the other hand, mature faster and can reach for control over their life sooner than boys.

We stopped walking into Sam's bedroom without knocking when he turned fourteen. It wasn't a conscious choice *per se*.

My conversations in his room changed from "Do you want me to read you a book?" to "Open the window; this place smells like a gym."

For kicks, I added, "Did you clean your jacks yet?" [3]

"No, I'm not doing that. It's disgusting."

"Well, neither am I," I said. "I'm afraid something would bite my hand off in there."

A boy, or young man, doesn't adjust to high testosterone levels until he reaches his early- to mid-twenties.

When I found that out, I tried forgiving myself for transgressions in my early twenties, like binge drinking and generally offering offensive opinions when no one asked.

Alas, my testosterone levels will continue to decline during my forties. Most middle-aged dads can go several days without thinking about sex and are contending with other fun personal crises like baldness and a high cholesterol level.

They Really Wanted That…

An older friend from work and his wife had a girl around the same time Sam was born. Two years later, his wife gave birth to another girl. I changed jobs and lost contact with him for a while.

One day, while out for a walk with Maria, I met my friend on the street pushing a buggy with a newborn baby girl.

"Congratulations," I said. "You went again?"

"We did!"

"Three girls, wow."

We went out for drinks the following weekend (us, not the babies). In the pub, he confessed his old school friends teased him.

"They tell me I've a sissy mickey," he said.

"What's a sissy mickey?"

"A penis that can't produce a son and heir." He threw his hands in the air and laughed. "I live in a house full of women!"

"I went to an all-boys school," I said. "I don't think my friends and I ever learnt how to talk to women until we were twenty-two and out in the real world. I'm still learning."

Some parents with a house full of boys or girls try one more time for the other sex... but more of the same isn't always the same.

And that's OK.

My friend seems happy living in a home with three girls and his wife. Last I heard, he's coaching his daughter's camogie team.[4]

Takeaways

Every guy forms unconscious biases about other groups of people, and that includes girls and boys. Becoming a dad exposes you to some biases about both sexes. Think of a gender stereotype you grew up with. Was it a conscious or unconscious choice on behalf of your parents? And did it hold truth or set limits for *you* and *your* family?

A dad might watch his daughter building a Lego tower and say, "It's beautiful." He tells his son, building the same Lego tower, "That's so high!" Or a dad and his daughter see a puppy on the street, and he says, "Look at that cute puppy." He sees the same puppy with his son and says, "What an awesome dog."

Perhaps it's best to draw a line between what responsible adults or elves feel girls and boys *should* enjoy and what the little people in our lives like. Some *girls* will wreck *your house* and some *boys* will wreck *your head*.

Personality runs deeper than gender.

PC Tips

- Instead of choosing "that's for boys" or "that's for girls", decide based on pursuits your son or daughter enjoys rather than what society (and the thought police) say is correct.
- Apply the same inquisitive mindset when considering other people's kids, too, i.e. ask a parent if they'll like your gift before buying it.

THIRTEEN

FRIENDS WITH KIDS

How long is a friendship?
One night
Half a lifetime ago

It's easy for a young guy without kids to maintain casual friendships, but becoming a dad forces a reckoning with unrewarding relationships.

Despite Mark Zuckerberg's best intentions, we didn't evolve enough to manage meaningful relationships with tribes larger than 150 people.

As a footloose and fancy-free young guy without kids, it's easy to maintain friendships with multiple groups of people. He can join disparate groups and tribes in college, at work or the office and try on identities as he sees fit. He can form friendships in the moment at no substantial cost. Together, a group can fill a small room.

But when friends pair up and pop out one, two, three and even more kids, a tribe rapidly shoots past 150 and splinters into smaller groups. Replace the small room with a town hall. Unless you're Bill Clinton, it's all but impossible to remember everyone's names and birthdays without the help of a CRM system. If a guy can track the number and ages of kids in their friends' families, he's doing better than most.

I settled on an easy rule.

Always remember the firstborn's name. It's enough of an ice-breaker to open up and talk about number two or three.

After all, if you can remember who won the Premier League or the Super Bowl five years ago, is it so hard to remember your mate's firstborn?

But if your memory fails, default to an open-ended question: "How's the family?"

Then listen carefully for any clues about their new tribe before the conversation swiftly changes.

Perhaps women are better at keeping track of their friends' expanding tribes.

Assemble a group of new mothers, and they'll peer into each other buggies, swap milestone stories about nappy rashes, teething problems, teeth, what time the baby got up at and who woke first – mam or dad.

Assemble a group of new dads, and they'll hurry past the buggy and "How's the family?" to golf games, football scores or (in my circle) running times.

Some good friends take a genuine interest in the latest escapade of their friend's son or daughter. But, if the parent stretches these stories too far, they'll snap like an elastic band.

Two parents might love swapping stories about the cute way their one-year-old daughter says "Nom nom time!" before dinner. Once is probably enough for friends, though.

Probably zero.

Your kids are cute; other people's less so. They've a bad habit of asking the same questions over and over and explaining when they're not getting what they want.

Dad anecdotes about the tooth fairy and toilet training get short shrift at the gym or in the pub. By all means, mark important milestones with family and some close friends, but don't expect non-blood witnesses to rouse the same excitement.

They're busy managing their own family's birthday parties, life events, and nom-nom times.

Even other dads sometimes want to meet up to forget all about the strife and worries of family life.

Unwanted Visitors

After a big college deadline years ago, the class decided on a celebratory night out. Our average age was about nineteen, and drinking money was in short supply. So, we loaded up on cans of cheap Dutch Gold beer in a classmate's flat beforehand.[1] Later on, the Palace bar served us drinks for a euro.

I arrived hungover into college the next afternoon to find a few of my classmates gathered in the canteen, huddled over Styrofoam cups of cheap coffee and talking quietly.

"What happened?" I asked. "Did the results come out? Was it worse than expected?"

"Didn't you hear?" said Frank. "Mick didn't make it home last night."

"He what?" I said.

"He passed out on the street last night?" said a classmate.

"Did he get into a fight?" said a second.

"Is he sick?" said a third.

"I don't know, I don't know," said Frank. "I'm going to visit him later."

"Count me in," I said.

"Me too," said another.

That evening after class, half a dozen of us got the bus across town to visit Mick in St James's hospital.

When we walked into the room, Mick sat up in bed and pulled the sheets over his chest. He looked pale and tired, and a small bandage covered his left temple.

"I remember walking home. I didn't drink too much... and then I woke up here," he said.

"What did the doctors say?"

Mick looked down at his bedsheets.

"I'll be OK. They're keeping me in overnight for observation."

We stayed for about half an hour, circling around the previous night, but Mick couldn't or didn't want to give much away. Still, we walked out of the hospital feeling pretty good about ourselves.

He looks OK to me. How nice of us to visit a friend in hospital when he's sick.

Years later, with that friendship firmly in the rear-view mirror, I realised we visited Mick, as much out of novelty as concern.

We'd free time after class and nothing else to do. Mick, with a white sheet, pulled up over his chest, and a bandage on his head, didn't need half a dozen casual friends bumbling through the hospital door to find out the latest.

When a guy is child-free, meeting a friend for lunch, dinner, coffee, or a pint requires a quick text. A guy's child-free days sometimes (but not always) overlap with life before adult responsibilities like a busy career, a mortgage and lasting relationships.

Combine raising a family with the inevitable baggage of life beyond the early twenties and meeting a friend takes weeks of planning.

Partners need to informed or invited, babysitters, arranged and an agreeable venue selected.

Casual friendships fall by the wayside.

As they should.

Still, a new parent knows who their good friends are, even if they don't see them as much as they'd like.

Today, I'd only visit a sick friend in hospital if it were serious... and even then, I'd call ahead and ask them, "Do you want us to visit?"

Turning up anyway, that's the family's job.

What Did You Say About My Kids?

Family let each other know what they're unhappy about and who's at fault, *ad nauseam*. A good friend, on the other hand, tempers these inclinations.

I met Rog and a few close friends for beers one Saturday evening. These were the people I wanted to spend time with and not casual acquaintances from college.

As a dad, it's not always easy to see close friends. We've to juggle our social life with a partner's, potentially hire a babysitter and also plan around the kids emerging social lives.

Out of our group, only two of us had kids, but the others were on the brink. So we swapped horror stories for our child-free friends.

Jay grumbled about his weekends being busier than a normal working week.

"I've to drop the three of them to football training and matches every Saturday and Sunday. It takes up the entire day. By the time Monday comes around, I'm bollocksed."[2]

Then it was my turn:

"Sam is going through a bout of temper tantrums," I said.

"What's he doing?" said child-free Rog.

I explained how Audrey and I were finding it hard to put Sam to bed and get him up on time for school each morning without pulling out my thinning hair.

"He doesn't like taking no for an answer," I said.

"Old Collins was a bit like that," said Jay.

I embellished a few details, and my story raised a few laughs and commiseration.

"He sounds like a mouth,"[3] said Rog, a few pints deep.

He meant little by this off-hand comment, and I was the one who complained about Sam's behaviour. But I wanted commiseration, not judgement. I wanted to punch my friend in the nose. *What gives him the right to criticise or make fun of my kids?*

I figured out why I was angry with Rog through a quick thought experiment.

Let's say two families with small kids meet up for lunch. If a child from family A starts throwing plates around the restaurant, the worst thing a parent from family B can do is discipline the wayward child.

My thesis: to criticise or discipline another child in front of their parents screams, "You're a lousy parent. I'm going to step in and show you how *we* do things better around here." Nobody likes that. It's hard enough figuring out the correct approach to disciplining a child with a partner, never mind with a friend.

So the next time you meet up with your friends and they start complaining about their kids, lend a sympathetic ear and laugh at all the right parts. Agree it's stressful, funny or unfair. And if you've got kids of your own, feel free to trade war stories from the front line.

Takeaways

As a new dad, you won't have as much free time to spend with casual acquaintances and half-hearted friends. You'll also have a little less in common with friends who've no kids. Not every friend without kids will understand or even take more than a passing interest in your son or daughter's latest escapade. Chances are they'll want to spend their time staying out all night, sleeping in late and hooking up.

Growing apart from some friends might be difficult to accept, but parenting works on guys in unexpected ways. One day you'll look around and discover you're not the same guy who enjoyed drinking six cans of Dutch Gold for a fiver in a field with his mates after school or bungee jumping off a hundred-foot crane hanging over a beach in Thailand. That doesn't mean forgetting what it's like to be a regular guy outside of nappies, school runs and family dinners.

It's OK to want to meet up with a few friends and sit in a quiet coffee shop or pub, catching up on who's going bald in a warm and comfortable room together.

Becoming a dad is a good opportunity to reevaluate the relationships in your life too. Who do you really enjoy spending time with? And what friendships are long past their sell-by-date? Spend more time with the former and less with the latter. Your close friends and family will thank you for it.

It's fashionable for modern parents to shun authority and try to become best friends with their kids. But, parenting isn't like a 1990s sitcom. Unless a son or daughter is an adult or has a family of their own, how can a parent serve as an authority figure and friend?

Play your role as dad with the kids and a friend with your mates.

Friends With Dad Jeans Tips

- Most friends get together around big calendar events like Christmas or Easter. With small kids, it's harder to meet up at these times, thanks to family commitments. Instead, arrange meet-ups with other dads weeks before or after the holidays.
- Become friends with another dad from your son or daughter's football or sports team. You'll spend a lot of the time on the sidelines either way. Plus, you can tag-team lifts to and from training or matches.

FOURTEEN
BIG WORDS

I've a pain in my top head.
I've a doody stuck in the gob.
All of these words, they're bloody odd.

Teaching kids how to talk is fun. It's also disconcerting to watch them express opinions and try on their own identities.

"I can't go to school today, Dad," said Maria one Monday morning.

"Why not? What's wrong?"

"I've a pain."

"Are you OK? Where is it?"

She tapped her temple and frowned.

"It's in my top head."

She's long since learnt the meaning of forehead, but I still take delight in asking, "How's your top head?"

Another evening, the kids sat down to watch Robin Williams in *Mrs Doubtfire*. When the credits rolled, Sam asked, "Dad, when you watched *Mrs Doubtfire*, was it in black and yellow?"

One Friday, I walked into the baby's room.

"Morning all."

He pulled himself up on the cot bars.

"A poo," he said.

"Really?"

He grinned.

"A big one."

"Yikes!"

It's fun teaching small kids how to talk. They've an odd way of mangling, confusing and misusing everyday words and concepts.

Newspeak[1] in our house, or at least with me, comprises obscure and old words.

When Audrey washed Sam and Maria's faces when they were babies, she sang songs like, "This is how you wash your face, wash your face on a cold and frosty morning."

I'm not much of a singer. So, I took a wet facecloth and told him, "This is how you wash your gob, wash your gob, come on now, all the boys are doing it."

Or, with toothbrush and paste in hand, I said, "Get over here; it's time to wash your choppers."

One evening K watched me come in from work, thought for a moment, and then waved at his mouth.

"No gob!"

His aunt was sitting at the kitchen table drinking coffee with my wife. Overhearing the exchange, she asked: "How can you teach him those weird words?"

How could I not!

For the first ten or fifteen years of a child's life, parents define what their kids say and how they say it.

A daughter says something her dad disagrees with, so he explains what's what. A son swears at dinner, and his father sets him straight. Or perhaps he lets the bad language pass and agrees with his daughter. The child learns from either approach about what they should and shouldn't say.

Shaping the language kids use to communicate carries a lot of parental power, but it's also a lot of responsibility.

I enjoy experimenting with language, though. Words are constructs built on shared viewpoints and experiences. I keep a file on my computer of weird words to bamboozle the kids with as they grow older. I imagine growing my beard into a pointy triangle that touches my chest and my daughter telling me, "Dad, you need a shave."

"It sounds like you've a bad case of pogonophobia."

"A what?"

"Haven't you heard? An extreme fear of beards."

I want them to understand the narrow viewpoints we approach language from. A child learns how to speak at home. They relearn how to talk to friends, and later with work colleagues or a partner or any time they join a new group.

Several years ago, I travelled around Argentina with three friends. One Saturday night, we got into a cab.

"Where you go?" said the driver.

"Wherever there's craic!" I said.

"Crack?" He sniffed his nose, spoke rapidly in Spanish and tapped at his map. "Si! Si!"

Then he winked at us and exaggerated a deep snort.

In Ireland, "craic" is a casual word describing harmless fun, whereas in other countries "crack" has class-A connotations. Two words that sound identical split by context and two letters.

The narrow viewpoint of a child widens as they become teenagers and start breaking out of houses in the middle of the night. They try on new identities and angle for a brief life outside the shadow of their parents.

After Sam finished some end-of-year exams, he insisted on going to a local GAA disco one Friday night with his friends.

I was against the idea from the start. I wanted to hold on to the clear boundaries I'd set a year or so previously – before my son had the tenacity to turn fourteen and sprout facial hair.

"You're too young. It's not happening," I told him.

"But everyone else is going. I've already bought the ticket. This is so unfair."

"I know for a fact your friend Cian isn't going," I said.

Sam likes to present his own version of alternative facts.

"Everyone else is," he said.

"You can't stop him forever," said Audrey.

So, I drove my son and three of his friends to a local GAA club on Friday night. On the drive over, one of them cracked a joke I couldn't follow. Everyone in the car, except me, laughed. I pulled up outside the front gates of the disco and let them out.

"Have a good night, lads," I said.

"We will," said my son.

I turned the car around, parked up on the verge, and watched them from the rear-view mirror.

"Keep walking, lads," I said. "All the way inside."

Nobody will sneak out on my watch!

Another Friday evening, I picked Sam and his compadres up. I was annoyed by his social life, leagues ahead of mine.

So, I got down to business.

"Evening, gentlemen," I said, the smell of cheap Lynx and hormones filling the car. "All in! Now let's head back to the gaff."

"The what?" said Sam.

"Gaff, it's another word for house... haven't you and your gang heard of the good word?"

His friends sniggered while Sam shook his head.

"Stop it, Dad," he said after I dropped them home.

"Stop what?"

"Where did you hear all these weird words, anyway?"

"Books," I said.

He frowned.

For a few years, Sam protested against books and reading: his personal Room 101. I took particular delight in acting like the Thought Police when I found gaps in his knowledge.

"You'll learn more in books than by looking at your blower twenty-two hundred times a day."

"My what?"

"Blower... the thing you spend your life on. Your phone."

"Oh my God. Let me out."

"Just in time." I turned into the estate. "Here's the gaff now."

Perhaps a disposition towards words harks back to when I was about nine or ten. The intricacies of pronouncing the "th" sound confounded me. "This, that, these, and those" turned into "dis, dat, dese and dose".

A teacher mentioned my stutter in passing to my mother, who promptly enrolled me in speech and drama classes. I fought with her for days about going.

"It's after school. Why do I have to waste my time there!?"

"You need to learn how to speak properly," she said.

"Dad?"

"Ask your mother."

So, every Monday evening, I sat on a small wooden chair for an hour reciting limericks, tongue twisters and poetry aloud, like: "They thankfully think this thing is the best thing that they can throw the three times they need to throw a thing."

"Slow down," the speech and drama teacher told me. "Sound it out."

I gradually learned to annunciate, elongate and break words into syllables. I took part in debates at school, first in English and later in Irish. A few years later, our year-head even asked me to deliver a graduation speech.

If this sounds like an odd cocktail of my mother, speech and drama classes, and the Gaeltacht transformed me into an exaggerated extrovert with a Churchillian grasp of oratory. Far from it. Writing and public speaking are ideal pursuits for classic introverts. It's you alone, talking or writing. And no one can interrupt.

Rites of Passage

It's one thing for kids to speak up about what they want and don't want at home. It's quite another for them to find rising confidence in the real world. Kids and teenagers can try on new identities and shed old ones without big consequences – adults, less so.

I could be bookish and nerdy in school. Or I could be the kind of guy who sneaks out in the middle of the night for an illicit party in a wet field. With three kids, I've lost some of that flexibility.

If I arrived home now with nose piercings and a

mohawk, it'd raise more than a few eyebrows.

For a few years, Maria was talkative at home but quiet in company. Before social situations, Audrey prompted her, "Use your big words."

These days, Maria is exploring her own way of stepping out from the shadow of her parents, of speaking up. She decided to run for class rep last term, with no prompts from us. The teacher asked every candidate to give a speech to the class, like miniature politicians setting out their manifesto.

I read Maria's big stump speech the night before.

"You're going to promise the class a pet?"

"Yes," she said. "A rabbit!"

"They'll love that," I said. "You have a real chance of winning here."

I wasn't the only one who read her notes.

On the day of the big vote, her best friend set out a bold manifesto to the class:

"If you elect me as your class rep, I promise to get the class a rabbit. A real one!"

She won on the first count.

"It's not fair!" my daughter said after dinner that night. "I was going to say that."

"It sounds like Doublespeak to me," I said. "Sometimes you've got to keep the best ideas to yourself. Only tell them when it feels right."

Takeaways

A baby over six months recognises basic words like "yes" and "no". By the time they turn three, they can understand hundreds of words and follow directions and instructions. *Can* doesn't mean *will*!

Small kids soak up your beliefs and express them back to other people in surprising and sometimes embarrassing ways. For example, if you swear about the delivery guy who threw an Amazon parcel over the front wall or the granny driver who cut you off in traffic, they will too.

It's natural to want to protect your kids and advocate on their behalf in the wider world. But they need a way of expressing themselves with their friends and peer groups, even if you don't like or understand what they have to say.

Encourage your kids to take responsible personal risks. Reward them when they try, not when they fail or succeed. Allow them to try on different identities and make safe mistakes of their own.

Wordy Tips

- Every child learns to speak at a different rate, but boys usually lag behind girls. Reading picture books together, encouraging them to sound out one- and two-syllable words, and even using signs, all prompt speech. On the other hand, baby talk and made-up words may hold them back.
- When your son or daughter wants to go to a disco, check who's going, what the other parents are doing, what time it starts and ends. Establish clear ground rules beforehand.
- If your son or daughter is active on social media, try this: "Don't post anything on any network or send anything online to your friends that you'd have no problem with me reading on a giant billboard outside the front of our house."

FIFTEEN
ROUTINES

I look back; it makes sense.
You look ahead, no consequences.
Today, here, we meet.

———————

Routine and structure are a dad's best friends, offering safe confines within which kids can thrive.

While transitioning from a regular guy to a struggling dad, I faced an unexpected challenge: balancing routine with spontaneity.

Before:

I argued at length for decriminalising every type of drug, getting rid of the Irish indoor smoking ban and tossing the government, any government, out of office.

I moaned about the hoops Irish homeowners faced, like

purchasing mandatory household insurance and mortgage protection.

I disliked and distrusted authority. I said to anyone who listened, "What gives them the right to tell us what to do? They're in our way. We should be able to do what we want when we want!"

"Them" being anyone in charge at the time.

After, I discovered some laws are sensible. Toss out the incompetent government, but it's best to keep speed limits in residential zones and some taxes, so the unemployed (like me) can claim social welfare.

I also discovered that dads are joint chiefs of the family operation for a few short years.

A baby needs a bottle, a nap, and for someone to hold them. Kids of all ages respond well to structure, and it's a dad's job to create it – even if he doesn't have a clue how to arrange his own day or week, much less a little person's.

As they grow older, you and your partner will play these roles: personal assistant, counsellor, cook, chauffeur, teacher, chef, doctor, nurse and protector.

It's a lot, right?

Gone Fishing

One November, we'd a big team meeting in the Dublin office. At the time, I was working as a copywriter for a large software company.

Team members flew into Dublin from London, Newcastle, New York and Atlanta.

Living an hour from the office, I'd no excuses for being late. If the team could fly across the world and turn up on time, surely I could negotiate heavy Dublin traffic and arrive at the office for a nine a.m. start?

The big team meeting coincided with a trip abroad for Audrey. I'd learnt the hard way previously. So, I got the kids ready for a busy morning the night before. I checked our new family car, a Kia Sportage, had enough petrol and left the car keys on the hall table next to my bag for work. I also prompted the kids to lay out their school uniforms and prepped as much of the lunches as I could in advance. I even set two alarms.

Afterwards, I went to bed early so I wouldn't nod off in an afternoon meeting and enjoyed the sleep of my life. I didn't even need the alarm clocks to get up.

First, I woke Maria.

She buried her head underneath the pillow.

"I don't want to go to school today, Dad."

"Why not?"

"I've a pain."

"Where?"

"Um, in my tooth?"

"You look fine to me." I turned on the lights. "Get out of that bed and come down for breakfast. We can't be late."

"This is so unfair."

So far, so good, I'd allowed enough time for minor contingencies like mysterious body organs gone awry.

Next, I woke the baby. He'd moved out of our bedroom and into his own a few months ago.

Knock. Knock. Knock.

"Is K-man in there?"

He laughed from inside.

"Will I come in?"

A baby has no sense of privacy, but I found this little morning game amusing.

Downstairs, I was pleasantly surprised to find Sam hunched over some school books at the kitchen table.

"You're up early?"

"I've a maths exam to get ready for."

I was less enthused to discover he'd used the last of the milk.

"What am I supposed to give the baby?"

K wiggled in my arms.

"A hot bop-bee?"

"That fella is always drinking milk," said Sam. "It's wasted on him."

"He's a baby," I said. "Drinking milk, that's his job."

Audrey left powdered milk at the back of the press for emergencies like these. Crisis adverted.

"I can't get the toast out," said Maria.

"Stick a fork in it," said Sam.

"A fork?" she said.

"Don't electrocute yourself," I said.

"But the toast is burnt," said Maria.

"That happens."

After breakfast, I picked up a thermos cup of coffee with one hand and the baby with the other.

Half-seven. Even allowing for heavy traffic, I'd more than enough time to drive across town.

"Don't forget to leave for school on time," I said to Maria.

"I won't."

"Good luck in your exam, Sam."

I opened the front door onto our driveway. The driveway was empty. I plopped the baby down on the ground and walked back inside.

There must be some mistake. Did Audrey come home in the middle of the night to take the car? Did I park around the corner? I don't think so... Did I leave the key in the front door last night?

Shit. Shit. Shit.
They've robbed it.

I rang the guards and my boss. She was more than understanding about the episode.

"Don't worry, once the kids are safe," she said.

A few hours later, a neighbour shared security camera footage recorded by his home camera at two in the morning. The video showed two thin, gangly men wearing hoodies, gloves and thick coats walking through the estate with fishing poles.

With insights from the guards and the security video, we pieced together what happened. The thieves stuck the fishing pole through our letterbox, fished the car keys off the hall table, opened the car, rolled the car down the driveway with the engine off and drove into the night.

Car theft is an extreme example of a stressful morning. But on a bad day, parenting kids is a little like running an increasingly demanding non-profit with no pay or health benefits. Expect many recurring jobs, like wiping off their finger prints from the inside of the car windows, cleaning dried Weetabix off the carpet or looking for the TV remote control batteries.

The job description says nothing about adjudicating over who gets to use the Wi-Fi and for how long. Like it or not, you're also expected to stay within budget too. Otherwise, expect a friendly call from a bank manager or landlord and several disappointed little faces come Christmas time or holidays.

On bad mornings, I swear at the kitchen toaster and complain about the kids running late. Occasionally, I lock myself in the bathroom, look in the mirror and tell myself, "I'm so far behind, how will I ever get any work done today?" and "Wow, you're going really grey."

I'm hardly a neurosurgeon. Every parent deals with these minor daily frustrations.

Usually, I march back out with fresh instructions.

Stop fighting.

Unplug the toaster first.

Have a good day.

Erect Scaffolding

Jerry Seinfeld leaves his toothbrush in the same spot in the bathroom each day, so he doesn't have to think about it. Obama wore the same-coloured suits while president, so he didn't have to worry about decision fatigue. Perhaps they can come around to my house and help out. On more than one occasion, I've caught myself wandering by the frozen vegetables in Tesco in a t-shirt that the baby vomited on as I took him out of the car.

The problem is you'll spend a year figuring out and creating a routine that works for everyone, and then the kids have the tenacity to go ahead and grow out of them.

When Sam got his first phone, he spent a lot of time playing games and watching YouTube at night. So we created (OK, *enforced*) a routine whereby everyone left their phone on a shelf in the hall every night before bed. This new routine didn't solve all problems a smartphone introduces into a family, but it reduced the number of times we got into an argument about staring at devices late at night.

It's one thing to say you're going to be an open-minded, patient, and tolerant parent. It's another thing to practice it after working a sixty- or seventy-hour week if you're worried about money and a partner has a different idea about managing the kids' latest escapades.

Perhaps if I wear the same t-shirt, wear the same pair of

socks or eat the same breakfast of porridge and fruit every morning, I'll get this house under control.

Perhaps not. But the kids' routines serve as scaffolding around which I can erect the rest of the day.

It took me a long time to build the level of patience parenting demands and accept routines aren't only OK; they're necessary.

That means getting up at the same time each day (babies are wonderful for this), and when work intervenes, negotiating with a partner about who gets to work and when. We even keep a whiteboard in the kitchen to map out the week and keep track of football matches, dance practice, exams and everything in between.

If I'm still behind, looking at my long to-do list and saying, "I don't have time for that one" or "this one never made sense" helps.

I still like grumbling about daily chores and reminiscing about being twenty-one and doing what I liked when I wanted.

On a good day, I remember I'm helping to create an actual person. So, I prefer establishing as many routines as possible with the kids. They mean I'm less stressed about if it's time to get up and get the kids ready for the childminder, playschool, the creche or school. I can start work or take the day off, mostly on time.

Screw spontaneity.

Think of it this way: even a wild plant needs some earth to latch onto.

Takeaways

After your baby arrives, expect to live life in blocks of four hours: sleeping, feeding, winding, and changing (them, not you). The days of sipping mojitos and watching the sun set are over, at least for a little while. When your child gets older, expect to spend time playing their personal executive assistant, ferrying them to their friends' houses, football training, dance practice and their chosen activities.

If managing the weekly schedule becomes an issue at home, or you catch yourself arguing with your partner about it, plan out the week or month in advance. Free time is a rare commodity for young families.

Kids like to know where you are, when's dinner and how long they can stay up (don't believe idle promises about staying up for another five minutes and still getting up on time for school the next day). They also like it when one or both parents are present to see them off or home from school.

Teenagers are interested in your whereabouts, too, if only to see what they can get away with. Even they like having boundaries they can throw themselves, or a few eggs, at.

Creating a family routine and structure reduces the dozens of little decisions and minor conflicts dads negotiate every day. Get it right and delightful moments will burst through everyday experiences, like sunflowers in a pot.

Tips for Creating Lasting Routines

- Set up a whiteboard in the kitchen or a shared digital calendar that everyone uses. That way, your growing family can write down their activities for the week. Plus, you'll know where they are (or at least where they're supposed to be).

- Understanding your partner or their mother's schedule is key. Sit down once a week with your partner and the kids, if they're old enough. Ask who wants to do what and when. Write it down (teenagers have selective hearing). It'll help everyone avoid stressful surprises.
- Exercise consistency because kids hate unfairness. If you, an older brother or sister is allowed to break the rules, they won't understand why they've to follow them.

SIXTEEN

DISCIPLINE

Running on his tippy toes,
Alive with chubby red cheeks,
I'll catch him.

Kids respond well to structure and rules. Family life is easier and more enjoyable for everyone, with a little discipline.

If I talked back to my mother while growing up, she sometimes picked up the Hoover brush and smacked me gently on the back of the legs.

It didn't hurt much, but the message was clear: behave or else!

My experience was hardly unique.

When I told a friend about my encounters with the Hoover, he confessed his mother "clipped me on the arse with a wooden spoon".

We had it easy.

In Ireland, most kids in school during the 1950s and 1960s, including my parents, faced corporal punishment. An empowered teacher walloped them with a ruler if their homework contained a mistake or they weren't paying attention.

These days, smacking a child, however gently, would capture the attention of social services. And shouting at kids to "stop it, the pair of you before I lose my mind!" is rapidly going the same way as smacking.

Babies don't stay cute babies forever, though. So what's a parent to do when their offspring morphs into a roaring, rule-breaking monster for few hours or if World War III breaks out between siblings?

What Do You Mean "Bring the Baby With Me"?

One sunny Sunday afternoon, a child-free friend invited our gang over to his new house for a BBQ.

"I've already got plans," said Audrey. "I told you about it last week."

"I haven't seen my mates in ages," I said.

"Why don't you bring the baby with you?"

"Are you joking?"

I packed a bag of nappies, bottles and changing wipes and drove our old Renault Clio to my friend's house.

Once Sam, now four, got into my friend's house, his eyes glazed over like a Blofeld plotting world domination, and he pulled free from me.

While I said hello to my friends, Sam ran from room to room, snatching food off the table, throwing empty cans on the ground, jumping on chairs and causing general havoc.

"How's it going, little man?" said Aidan. "You're after getting big." [1]

"I want some." Sam pointed at the chocolate biscuit on his paper plate.

Before Aidan replied, Sam snatched two and ran off.

"He's some lad," said Aidan.

"He keeps us busy," I said. "I don't get a minute."

My plan for a quiet Sunday catchup morphed into running after Sam, checking he was safe and not breaking anything valuable. My friends took particular delight in the situation.

"Look at Collins," said Aidan. "I can see the beads of sweat forming on his head."

"It couldn't happen to a nicer person," said Nigel, sipping his beer. "I'm never having kids."[2]

After an hour of running around after Sam, I picked him up.

"Lads, I'm off, I'm done. I can't hack it anymore."

I frogmarched him out of the house and strapped him into the car seat. He cried, and I felt like joining him. I was hot, sweaty and frustrated. I vowed never to bring a small child to an adult event again.

In the car, I turned around to Sam and launched into a tirade.

"You were a very bold boy in there. You're supposed to do what I say. Never, ever run around like that again."

He looked at me blankly.

"Are, are you even listening to me?!"

He pulled off his shoe, held it up into the air and inspected it.

"Where's Mammy?"

I sprouted a few grey hairs that afternoon, but I could

only explain so much to somebody who'd only clocked up forty-eight months on the planet.

Ironically, the weekend before, while at the Playzone, he'd done the same thing. Except for that time, he was in a controlled environment for kids, where they expect this type of behaviour. And afterwards, in the car, I'd told him, "You're a great boy!"

How was a four-year-old supposed to distinguish one from the other? It was my fault for placing inconsistent expectations on his growing shoulders. Sam, like many busy boys his age, thrived on consistency.

Anything else was a recipe for a meltdown.

How Not To Send a Toddler Into Time-Out

When Sam was small, we relied on the help of grandparents, aunts and childminders.

Family were understanding, but it's an odd thing to leave your child with a stranger, get into the car and go about the day, knowing he's having experiences he can't tell you about.

It's also unusual to cycle through nine childminders in a few short years.

We settled on one childminder who lived a ten-minute walk from home. After a few months, she called around one evening, wanting to speak to Audrey.

"Audrey's out for the night," I said.

"Can I come in, anyway?" she said.

We sat in the living room.

"This house is lovely," she said.

"Have you not been here before?"

And then it came:

"I don't have the energy for Sam. I'm so sorry, I can't

take him anymore. He's just so busy, and my daughter has exams."

It was like being dumped for the first time.

Another childminder had an odd way with Sam. She greeted me at the front door before I could knock and plopped him at my feet.

"He's had another bad day, Bryan."

She handed me a plastic bag with a pair of jeans and a dirty nappy. I held the bag up and away from my nose.

One for the bin.

"He's toilet training... we're having difficulties. What can I do?" I said.

"That's not my problem. I can't change him. I can't teach him. I've other kids to mind too."

"It's not working out then, is it?"

A third childminder left Sam sitting in front of the TV while her family sat down for dinner.

"Oh, I don't like feeding them. I let them graze all day."

What, like cattle?

"Is it us?" I said to Audrey one evening, while in between childminders five and six.

Sam stood in front of the TV watching *Power Rangers* shouting at the top of his lungs, "It's morphing time!"

"Is it him?"

"Of course not," she said. "He's such a good boy."

"He gets worked up about things," I said. "When he gets an idea into his head, he can't let it go."

"I wonder where he gets that from *Bryan*," said Audrey.

Sam climbed up onto the couch and jumped off, waving an imaginary sword in the air.

"He's certainly energetic," I said.

When Sam's granny visited, he chased her around the sitting room or hid behind a pillar and jumped out in front of her laughing. He loved taking people's keys from their handbags and hiding them in his bedroom. We told her about a recent episode where he kicked the washing machine door in a temper, and she recommended trying the time-out approach.

After an eventful dinner one night, we faced an inevitable stand-off over bedtime.

"You deal with him tonight," said Audrey. "See how he is."

"I don't want to go," said Sam.

He threw his juice on the ground and smashed the cup.

"That's it!" I said. "Get up to bed *immediately*."

I carried him out of the living room and upstairs to his bedroom at the top of the house.

"Get in there, sit on the bed and have a think about what you did," I said. "Is it really OK to throw your cup on the floor like that?"

"I want my Mam!"

He kicked his red Power Ranger across the room. When he tried to run past me to the door, I grabbed his arm and plonked him back down on the bed.

"You're going into a time-out."

"I won't do it, Dad! Let me go. You're hurting me!"

He barged past me towards the door.

"No way, you can't make me, no way, no way, no way!"

I ran after Sam, caught him on the stairs and walked him back while he kicked, screamed and slapped me.

"Get off me, Dad."

"Time-out! I swear to God..."

I sat him on the bed, ran out of the room and slammed his bedroom door. He kicked it from the inside.

"My foot, my foot," he cried. "It hurts."

When I opened the door, he hopped past me crying and ran downstairs.

"I'm telling Mam about you."

"Fine, do what you want," I called after him. "I've had enough."

I found him downstairs, sitting on his mother's lap, reading a book.

"Why were you fighting with him?" Audrey asked. "That's not the way to go about it."

His eyes were red and wide.

My eyes darted from Sam hugging his mother to the broken dinner plate underneath the table.

I walked out of the house and stood at the entrance to our estate, breathing in and out.

I'm supposed to be the adult here. Why is this so bloody hard?

Laissez-faire Parenting

Boys act out when they need help from their parents, whereas girls are more likely to ask for it. As I mentioned in a previous chapter, it's also normal for small boys to experience a burst of testosterone around four or five. These bursts manifest in energetic moments, like chasing a Granny with missing keys around the living room or a troubling standoff at bedtime.

If it sounds like Sam was a problem child, far from it.

During our early years parenting Sam, I was like a drunk loaded up on vodka fumbling around in the dark, searching for a light switch in a strange room. When we weren't mired in WWWIII, I tried (and usually failed) to drive our conversations like this:

Me: "Are you ready to talk?"

Sam: "Yes."

Me: "What did you do that I was cross about?"

Sam: "Throwing my dinner on the floor. But I didn't like it!"

Me: "That's OK, you don't have to eat it next time. Was there anything else?"

Sam: "Shouting at Mam."

Me: "Do you need more time to think about it?"

Sam: "I'm sorry."

That he's a responsible teenager now and (almost) a functioning member of society is more of a testament to his personality and Audrey's presence.

Kids don't come with an instruction manual. Time-out might work for child A, but it could send child B into a spiral he can't get out of. Child C might respond well to a firm voice and clear boundaries, but child D worries all night about getting into trouble with a strict parent. Each child is like a Rubik's Cube only a parent can solve.

Sam didn't respond well to power struggles, even if they were disguised as "time-outs". As he grew older, I turned to subtler techniques like redirection, reasoning and bargaining. I deployed stealth weapons from my parenting arsenal, like stopping their weekly allowance or adding more chores to their list of jobs. Shutting down the Wi-Fi early is my weapon of mass destruction.

With Sam, I sought a win/win middle ground. My more hands-off approach leads to many bargaining conversations.

"If you go to bed on time this week, I *might* get you the new FIFA game."

Or:

"If you stop pulling your sister's plaits, we'll stop for chocolate ice cream."

And:

"That's a question only your mother can answer."

Rewarding good behaviour is another popular self-discipline strategy.

"If you want to stay up late and watch football, I'd get your homework in first. But, hey, that's just me, and I don't even like football. The question is: what do you want to do?"

"I wanna see the game, Dad. I'll get the homework in."

Some criticised my laissez-faire parenting style. One family member said, "You use money too often as a crutch when they act up."

Another friend said, "Let a gentle roar at the young lad every now and again. He should know who's boss."

How could I explain discipline isn't a cookie-cutter affair?

Dads set explicit and implicit rules for kids about what's acceptable or unacceptable. Go around the house shouting at everyone, and the kids will too. Apologise quickly and easily, and they will take note. It's helpful if both parents at least agree on an approach, even if it's the wrong one. I say "if" because it's hard enough for one person to carry baggage from childhood into their new jobs, let alone someone else's.

The stakes rise as kids get older.

Questionable friends with questionable hairstyles. Bullies and bullying. Alcohol under the age limit. Cars driven at speed. Class A drugs. The front page of the Sunday papers.

When the ground rules are clear, it's easier to teach kids to choose correctly between vice and virtue. Otherwise, they'll exploit those weaknesses to get what they want, like a mini-rogue state at the UN.

When one of us is about to lose it, I remind myself kids

lack the same ability to regulate their emotions or blow off steam like adults.

Takeaways

You don't need to worry about discipline with babies. Thanks to a two-second attention span, they're easily redirected.

"Oh look, here's your Mammy! And she's brought a bottle of milk."

Toddlers and small kids are more fiendish. They easily spot when parents are inconsistent or unsure of the rules. And they love it when one parent says "No" and but the other says "Yes". But they don't respond well if a parent becomes angry or upset with them.

No matter how bad the outburst, you're the adult in the room. Telling them to stop crying seldom works and nor does shouting or smacking.

There is no excuse for getting physical with a child, no matter how bad the outburst.

However, it's OK to walk away sometimes instead of over-reacting. And if you lose it, apologise. It's a nice little teaching moment that helps your child process negative emotions when they're older.

It's much harder to manage minor challenges the little people in your life present without routine and structure because they thrive within them.

Deploy "No" early, often and gently.

Check on them when the house is eerily quiet, but don't expect everyone to understand if you play the occasional villain at home.

Parenting small kids quickly exposes differences of opinion between parents. Agree on ground rules with your partner beforehand... or after a particularly challenging day.

How will you both deal with a temper tantrum (theirs, not yours)? Is using time-outs OK?

For example, with K, we use a time-out step. As he's only two (at the time of writing this book), he sits on it for all of three seconds and only immediately after a temper tantrum. That's more than enough time for him to understand that he's done *something* he shouldn't have. My big mistake with Sam was expecting him to sit in time-out for far longer than he was capable of.

Whatever their age, avoid public situations where you'll end up correcting your kids often, like wandering around an antique shop or into an electronics store with chocolate-covered fingers.

When they're older, teach your son or daughter to think through their actions, apologise and move on.

Temperamental Toddler Tips

- Use colourful reward charts toddlers can pin stickers onto when they do something good. This tip works for toilet training too.
- Reward positive behaviours. Small kids (and many adults) respond well caught in the act of being good rather than facing criticism for breaking house rules: "What do you mean you have a dirty nappy? That's great news!"

SEVENTEEN
BULLIES

Fight me.
Fear me.
Wait, don't go.

———

Encountering a bully is an upsetting and difficult experience for kids. But it doesn't have to be that way for either party.

"Watch out for the Murrays!"

As kids growing up, we whispered this warning to each other every time we passed the shady house at the top of the cul-de-sac in our estate.

Mick, a year or two older than me and my friends, lived inside with his mother and three brothers. My friends and I were in terror and awe of the Murrays.

We'd no idea what happened to his father. Gardaí squad cards regularly called up to their house, and whispers went around the cul-de-sac about an older brother sent to prison.

One day, my friends and I were walking out of the cul-de-sac to the shop.

Our chief tormentor, Mick Murray, stepped out of his driveway with the purpose of a CIA interrogator.

"You must bow when you pass my house!"

"Bow when I pass your house? No way, Murray!" I said.

He punched me in the arm.

"If you don't show respect, I'll get you, Collins. I know where you live."

I rubbed my arm.

"I won't do it."

He pushed me to the ground. We rolled around for a bit until my two friends pulled him off. Murray was bigger than any of us, but we outnumbered him. So, he retreated into the dark hallway of his house like a wounded dragon.

I didn't see Murray for a few weeks after that. We played bulldog on the street most days and never saw him. He didn't attend the same school as us either.

One Tuesday evening, I was walking alone back from the school bus stop.

When I passed Murray's house, he jumped out from behind a bush and into my path.

"I've got you now, Collins! You walked right past, and you didn't bow to my house. I'll teach you some respect."

"Get off me, Murray!" I tried to push him away.

"What did you call me? I'm the king around here!"

He grabbed my school bag off my back, emptied the books and lunchbox onto the ground. Then he zipped down his trousers and urinated into my schoolbag.

After finishing, he handed me back the bag. The urine sloshed around inside.

"Get lost, Collins."

I walked in the backdoor of our house, upset. My explanation horrified my mother. After washing out the schoolbag with scalding water and disinfectant, she called up to his mother to complain.

I don't think she'd much luck, though.

Tackling Schoolyard Bullies

Parents worry about irrational things happening to their kids and events beyond their control. Either way, they can only do so much.

My mother worried a lot about bullies. For years after that incident with the Murray's, she sat my brother and me down every few months.

"Are you being bullied? You'd tell me if you were being bullied."

"No, Mam," my brother and I replied in tandem. "We're not being bullied."

I hated Murray as much as a kid can work up an emotional intensity against anyone after the incident with my school bag.

Oddly enough, an older boy urinating in my school bag was the nadir of childhood bullies. The worst had already happened. When I encountered them in secondary [1] school, later on, they didn't faze me as much as Murray.

Duck was one example. We were in the same class for few years in secondary school. Duck was the kind of guy who was the first to drink alcohol and smoke hash in our class. He was also one of the brave few to do it in the school bathroom.

Duck took a particular dislike to the way I glanced at him one morning in physics class. A certain glint in my eye that said, "I know a little more than you, and I'm better at it."

When the teacher left the classroom on an errand, Duck got in my face, "What are you looking at, Collins?"

"I don't know, Duck, but whatever it is, it's looking back."

The class erupted.

He punched me in the back of the head. I laughed it off, and Duck drew back again and punched me repeatedly in the arm. The more he hit me, the more I laughed. His punches hurt, but I got a kick out of his loss of control during a grey Tuesday afternoon in physics.

He drew back for a knockout punch in the head when someone called out "Sketch!"

That was our codeword for a teacher on their way. Duck's head darted around to the doorway in panic, his fist still raised.

"Stop that at once," the teacher said to him. "Take your bags and get down to the principal's office immediately!"

Duck and I didn't have any great rivalry. It was him versus whoever was in his way. The school suspended Duck a few weeks later for fighting with someone else in another class. Later on, they expelled him for a messy brawl in the hall.

The Brutal Truth About Bullies

My mother enrolled my brother and me in lifesaving classes because she worried about accidental drownings, too. We trained every Wednesday night in the local swimming pool.

I was terrified to discover Jack was taking the same classes. He was half a foot taller than the rest of us and all muscle. He came with a fearsome reputation as someone not to mess with.

Our parents dropped and picked us up from the swimming pool. Jack arrived and left as he pleased and always alone. I reckoned a weedy nerd like me would be bird food for him.

A large part of lifesaving training involves towing another person up and down the pool as if you're saving them from drowning. The would-be lifeguard swims on their side with an arm wrapped around the victim.

It's hard to fight with someone when you're playing at saving each other's lives.

Jack took particular delight one evening when I accidentally pulled another swimmer onto the steps instead of letting him go at the pool bank.

"Collins, you're crazy," he said.

"I wish you'd watch it," said Eoin, rubbing his elbow.

Jack and I partnered up most weeks after that. He wasn't so bad after all. Together, we passed several big exams.

"There's no stopping us now, Collins," he said afterwards.

Jack brought an odd combination of muscle and innocence to the pool.

One evening, he said, "Lads, I've got to leave the pool early tonight. I'm off to get a new jacket."

"Is your mam taking you out to buy one?" said Eoin.

"I don't think any shops are open now," I said.

"The ma? Nah, I'll head out to Leixlip to get one myself."

"But Collins is right," said Eoin. "The shops aren't open at this hour."

"Ah, I'll hop on some young lad and take it off him."

Was he joking? Who knew? But we all laughed anyway.

I worry about what will happen when our kids encounter bullies. But I worry more about kids turning into bullies. It's a parent's job to keep their kids safe.

The brutal truth about bullies is they have it the hardest. They're unable to form lasting friendships, face trouble at home or have a tenuous circle of friends and absent parents.

Sometimes, I think of Jack wandering the streets on a cold night, while I got into a hot car with wet hair, and my mother drove us home for dinner.

I think of Duck leaving school and falling further away from his peers while we graduated, travelled and found jobs.

Murray's family eventually moved out of the cul-de-sac where I grew up.

After they left, we whispered to each other that Gardaí raided their home for drugs, and they were on the run. I whispered the loudest. The house sat empty for a while. Finally, an older couple without kids moved in, and we forgot all about the Murray's.

We stopped playing bulldog. We grew up.

Pay No Attention to *The Sopranos*

One sunny Sunday afternoon, a few years ago, Sam got into a fight with another boy in our estate over a football. They kicked and punched each other. Everyone was OK, but the boy's mother was less than impressed.

I grounded Sam for the rest of the day.

"He's an asshole," said Sam.

It's shocking to see how hard kids are on each other

sometimes, but that's only because they haven't figured out how to express themselves properly yet.

"Don't use that language."

"I've done nothing wrong," said Sam, in tears. "He started it. He keeps taking my football."

Perhaps he was right. The other boy regularly got into fights with other kids on the street, and I often saw him and his younger brother roaming the estate alone after dark. From what I could see, the two boys didn't make friends with the other kids on the street easily.

Still, macho advice like "hit them back" only works in films and television shows. Tackling bullies isn't like a scene from *The Sopranos*.

"Stealing footballs doesn't give you the right to hit him back," I said. "If you told us, we could have asked his parents to give it back."

"I don't like him."

"You don't have to be friends with him," I said. "But fighting like that isn't OK."

He got up from the dinner table and stormed off to his bedroom.

That evening, I went out for a long run through the old town where I grew up.

Did I handle things right with Sam? How could I teach him to stand up for himself but also respect other boys? Was this the first incident or just the first one we heard about?

I didn't find any easy answers. It's one thing to negotiate conflict in our housing estate or school, but our kids' generation also has to contend with cyberbullying. I vowed to go home and install monitoring software on the family computer.

I ran by the old cul-de-sac where I grew up. Stopping at the Murray's front wall, I remembered all the times we played bulldog while Murray sat inside alone, how we laughed and spread rumours about the police calling up to his house and his dad leaving. I wondered what happened to him and if he's OK now.

Not every kid or teenager is.

I didn't see Jack much after we finished up with life-saving classes. I met him once or twice by chance on the street or in the pub. We'd stop and say hello and joke about lifesaving.

But our small talk was stilted. When I told Jack about college, he was vague about his plans. Our lives were set on different trajectories.

A year or two went by.

I forgot all about him. Then one night, I met a friend in the pub. He told me about Jack, that'd he hung himself one afternoon.

Takeaways

Every child encounters bullies in one form or another in the playground, at school, college and online.

Kids play one of three roles: the bully, the victim or the bystander. Unfortunately, you can't help them negotiate all these battles. Even if you could, becoming a helicopter parent[2] will do them a disservice later in life.

Teach your kids the skills to tackle bullies, like using humour, standing up for themselves without violence and reporting them to other authority figures. Learning how to ignore an insult or a call to fight works well too. Kids can defeat some bullies with mental smarts; and they might even make friends with a few. Explain bullies have issues of their own and experience the world from a much darker place.

Practising this type of empathy will help your son or daughter understand why they shouldn't treat more vulnerable people this way.

Gaslighting is another form of manipulative behaviour that's hard to identify without an explanation from a parent. For example, one teenager insults another about their weight. Later, they say, "I never called you fat. I'm your friend. You must have imagined it." They might even enlist the help of others to support their false version of events.

Finally, explain to your kids it's not OK to stand by and watch someone become a victim of bullying.

Tips for Dealing With Bullying

- Watch out for the physical signs of bullying like bruises and torn clothes. Pay attention when a son or daughter suddenly refuses to go to school or an activity, begins stealing money (to give to their bully) or withdraws from their social circle.
- It's normal for some boys to act out at home while performing well at school, or vice versa. Close that knowledge gap by talking to their teacher about your concerns.
- When people think of bullying, they imagine fights after school. Speak to your kids about these other common forms of bullying: excluding others from social activities, teasing, starting or spreading rumours, threatening to end a friendship.

EIGHTEEN

DAD SCIENCE

Let's have a baby.
Let's not.
We can't wait to tell everyone.

The skills a dad needs today aren't the ones he'll use tomorrow.

Money. Food. Sex.

A regular everyday guy spends a lot of free time daydreaming about how they can get more, with who and when.

A single cell, he's free of dependents and all associated worries and responsibilities.

New dads take heed of mitosis – the process of single cells splitting, dividing and growing until an organism takes on a life of its own. German biologist Walther Flemming came up with the term in 1882 to explain the cell cycle, and it's kind of like the stages of becoming a dad.

Unknowing Dad

An unknowing dad has comprehensive plans for *his* future. He may be in the last stages of booking a winter ski trip or have elaborate designs for turning the back bedroom into a games room.

Alas, his partner hasn't told him she's expecting a baby... yet. She might not know, or she's getting ready to produce a positive pregnancy test stick.

Either way, unknowing dad is about to swap *"His"* for *"Our"*.

And when she tells him, he doesn't know where to begin.

Expectant Dad

We may find expectant dad clutching the grainy black photo of a baby scan and pointing out why he's having a girl or a boy. A carbon copy of himself, he can't quite believe it. Sometimes expectant dad will enter a state of shock. So, extend a hand. Bring him out of it with phrases like "welcome to the club!"(All dads like clubs.)

Occasionally a more confident version of expectant dad will say things like "We're pregnant" and even confess to suffering from sympathy morning sickness.

Should this happen, explain to him in great detail the basics of human biology... with supporting pictures.

Useless Dads

Typically found in the labour ward, useless dad's role is to hold their partner's hand, know when to keep quiet and when to say "Push!"

Occasionally, we may give useless dad small errands like fetching a phone charger, sandwich or a fizzy energy drink from the hospital shop.

Now is not the time to regale his partner or the midwife with fun facts he picked up from *What to Expect When You're Expecting.* [1]

His primary function is to stay out of the doctor's way.

New Dad

We may find new dad surrounded by congratulations cards, sitting next to his partner and baby in a hospital bed or late at night by the crib.

Whereas before, he worried about dropping the baby, now he's taken aback by this new nucleus before him, with a life all of its own.

I made this!

Observe new dad closely, and you may spot him inhaling the smell of his baby's head.

He'll use phrases like "he sleeps a lot" or "she's so small".

He's right.

For now.

Confident Dad

Confident dad struts around the playground with the poise of a gazelle. He knows where his children are, their birthdays, their best friends, *their birthdays*, and he carries a shopping list in his pocket for this evening's dinner.

He may even don a stylish little baby harness so other dads can see he's got this parenting gig under control. Confident dad sets the rules, and he expects the kids to follow them.

Older versions of confident dad are often spotted driving people carriers with three or four kids between runs to school, football training or dance practice.

They've honed their planning skills with the precision of a military drill instructor.

Interrogated Dad

Interrogated dad faces endless questions, conundrums and dilemmas. Who knew navigating the minutiae of everyday life could be so perplexing?

A newbie interrogated dad tackles mind-benders like:

"Why did you and Mammy dress up like a prince and princess?"

And:

"Dad, why are some cows brown?"

He's grateful for the Internet.

A more experienced interrogated dad knows Google doesn't hold all answers. He's busy deciding how much of an allowance to pay his kids (if any), what to do when they get into a fight at school, and how to convince them to flush the toilet.

Hungover Dad

Hungover dad thought it would be fun to stay out an hour later or have one more drink with friends he hasn't had time to see in months.

He reasoned he can still get up early the next morning with the kids and persevere on a few hours of sleep using coffee as a crutch.

He was wrong.

Teenage Dad

Teenage dad doesn't understand it happened so quickly. One minute, his daughter was so small, and he was the centre of her world.

Now, she's telling him he doesn't understand style. He apparently doesn't get it...whatever *it* is.

He spends his days shepherding a hormonal fifteen-year-old from one activity to the next. When he applied for the job of dad, he didn't remember seeing "taxi driver" on the requirements list.

It surprises teenage dad to find he must knock before walking into his son or daughter's bedroom, even though he owns the place.

He's careful to give them time and space... but not so much that they raid the drinks cabinet and set the house on fire when he goes away for the weekend. His days are numbered. He knows his son or daughter is about to separate from him.

Until then, teenage dad uses phrases like "no," and "I said no!" and "ask your mother."

Veteran Dad

Veteran dad sits patiently through expectant dad's talk of trimesters. He nods when new dad explains how strong his son's little grip is. And he commiserates when hungover dad vows never to stay out late again.

He advises like Gandalf to Frodo, all the while thinking, *You have no idea what's still ahead.*

We recognize veteran dad by his streaks of grey hair (*if he has any left*) and a general look of world-weariness, an extra five years for every child.

Veteran dad has been at this for a while now. He doesn't need to explain. If parenting were a war, he'd have a Purple Heart. He knows the real purpose of his son or daughter: to replace his worn-out self.

We find him waving his son or daughter off to college... or packing their bags when they're thirty and have forgotten the time-sacred duty of every man-child to move the hell out.

I Can't Believe It! Dad

I can't believe it! dad thought he was done. He'd packed up the plastic baby toys and donated them to the charity shop. He'd said goodbye to bleary-eyed feeds at three a.m. He'd changed his last nappy and pushed his last buggy. His friends had even congratulated him on a job well done.

Then I can't believe it! dad's partner confessed she wanted another baby. Or she announced one evening after dinner, "I'm pregnant!"

I can't believe it! dad doesn't remember getting much of a say in the matter. Only this time, he knows where to begin.

Spectator Dad

Spectator dad's kids have all finally left for college, work and lives of their own.

Some would caution him about empty nest syndrome. Others would plan a party.

Also known as Granddad, he's happy to watch from the sidelines, he might even volunteer for the occasional stint as a babysitter, but he's free, free at last.

Don't Fight Biology

A dad transitions through many stages during his humble parenting career, sometimes forwards, sometimes backwards. Best not to over-identify.

Veteran dad becomes expectant dad, and I can't believe it! dad finds himself in the delivery room again, happy to change a lightbulb when the midwife asks.

One dad is content to watch his son or daughter grow. Another adds prodigiously to his brood. Money, food and sex might be on their minds, but both can barely remember when they had only themselves to care for.

A dad's role develops until his family, whatever its size or shape, becomes an organism all of its own. Such is biology.

Takeaways

Becoming a dad is rarely boring.

Kids go through different developmental stages: baby, toddler, preschool, school, early teenager and teenager. Refresh yourself on the basics.

Get comfortable with the shifting nature of your role.

Knowing how to change a nappy or wind a baby is a completely different skill to dealing with a temperamental toddler, let alone a teenager with mixed-up ideas about the facts of life.

When in doubt, get advice from a dad who's further along. Explain what stage you're at and the issues you're having. Ask them, "What's next?" Whatever the issue, someone in your circle can relate.

Approach parenting with a beginner's mind. The strategies that worked for your youngest won't necessarily transfer neatly to your next-born.

Tips (Caution: Not Backed by Science)

- Use "I'm getting up with a baby tomorrow" as an excuse to leave or even avoid social or work events you'd rather skip. On the flip side, if you're considering staying out late, remember minding a baby with a hangover is much harder than a normal day at the office.
- If the kids outnumber you, divide and conquer with your partner or their mother. It's easier to entertain kids of the same age.

NINETEEN

KEEPING SCORE

Want to cheat? Just press:
Up, up, down, down, left, right, left,
Right, B, A, and start.

Raising kids is a little like a video game. Some dads like playing to win. Others play for the sheer fun.

Many gamers know that sequence intimately. Known as the Konami Code, it's one of the most famous video game hacks of all time. Creator Kazuhisa Hashimoto, who died in 2020, built this code into the 1986 title *Gradius*, as the game was too difficult to play during testing. After inputting the code, players received all available power-ups.

Since then, games used the Konami Code to unlock Easter eggs in dozens of popular titles over the years, including *Super Street Fighter II Turbo*, *League of Legends*, and *Metal Gear Solid*. They turn to it when things get tough, and they want to reach the next level. It's helped me beat games I wasn't good enough to finish.

I've a theory: family life is like playing a rewarding yet increasingly challenging video game. Dads can play early and often with their son or daughter. When all else fails, they can even cheat.

Level One: Turning Up

At level one, it's good enough to turn up. When the practice gets tough, you can become a type of Konami Code for your child. A dad congratulates and motivates their offspring to keep them going. Expect kids to accumulate many participation awards at level one.

When Sam started playing hurling, he returned from matches and tournaments with certs, medals and trophies. He took pride in showing them off to his grandparents, aunts and uncles.

I'm not immune to playing at level one either. A few years ago, a local athletics club gave me an award for "Most Improved Runner".

I ran so slowly the previous year that any effort at all on my part represented progress. I didn't care. I put the plaque on the top shelf in my office. The following year, when I felt like an unfit failure, it motivated me to keep turning up at the track and push through to the next level.

You're unlikely to get a medal or an award for mastering the delicate art of changing nappies at three in the morning. But turn up enough, and the next level awaits.

Level Two: Establishing the Rules

A few years ago, Sam received a mixed mid-year school report. He scored well in subjects like English and Irish, but less so in Maths. And he was distracting other kids by talking during lessons. His teacher wrote, "Some of Sam's old habits can resurface from time to time, so he should work at them next term." He carried on, "Although Sam is a capable and competent young man, I feel he is not reaching his full potential academically due mainly to his lack of interest in his school work."

At first, I took the report as a personal slight on our parenting skills. I didn't agree with everything the teacher said. After all, Sam was an energetic seven-year-old. Hardly a court-martial offence to talk out of turn, but at level two, turning up isn't enough.

I put a moratorium on binging on *Power Rangers* TV after dinner, while Audrey rang the teacher to find out more.

"Your son is distracting other students by talking and joking while we're trying to work," the teacher told her.

School comes with many boundaries and rules for new players. I'm on board with that. In our family, kids thrive within a loose form of structure. For us, that meant deciding on mini-dilemmas like chocolate and *Power Rangers* after dinner, staying up late on Friday evenings and dealing with a negative report card.

Dads face hundreds of mini dilemmas while raising kids. There are many ways to play. They can defer them to a partner, revert to what their parents did, or carve a fresh path.

Whatever the choice, another set of parents believes in

the opposite approach. Ask, and they'll explain why at great length.

Level Three: Playing with Others

Sam joined a local football team one year. I've always hated football because I'm awful at team sports, but I brought him to training at the local club because my wife insisted.

"It's good for him," she said.

"But he's already playing hurling," I said.

"I want to do both," said Sam.

His team won their first few football matches of the season. Then, one Saturday morning, Sam tackled an opposing player about to score, knocking him onto the ground.

The referee raised a yellow card.

Sam raised his hands in the air and swore.

The ref raised a red card.

Sam stomped off the pitch, clenching his fists and muttering to himself.

I caught him on the sidelines.

"Is that any way to talk to..?"

"Stop it, Dad, you know nothing about football."

He had me on that one. He was also still angry and not in the right frame of mind for some of my patented life advice.

After the match, Sam's coach gave him a gentle dressing down. He explained what constituted good and poor behaviour from team players.

"If you want to get your game, show respect to the ref," said the coach.

Sam nodded while his teammates watched on and promised to do better next time.

Getting snippets of life advice from someone who wasn't a blood relative opened Sam's eyes a little to what the rest of the world expects. It turns out mams and dads aren't the only people with rules.

After that incident, talking back became more infrequent, and I enjoyed taking him to football. But an argument on the pitch is only one marker on his journey towards autonomy.

Level Four: Winning (or Losing) with Grace

"Parents, please no shouting from the sidelines. This isn't the All-Ireland Final."

That's what the sign read over the entrance to Naas hurling pitch. Sam's team were playing in a final against their arch-rivals.

Before the match, Sam's coach, a greying, large man in his late forties, produced a large felt marker and gathered his charges.

"Now, lads, I want each of you to give it your all today," he said. "Every buachaill[1] here, stick out your hands."

The coach produced a red felt-tip marker and scrawled "100%" on the forearm of every player. They stormed onto the pitch, shouting, clapping and roaring like fans at a WWE event.

During the match, the coach stood on the pitch sidelines, roaring at the team to "press on".

After a player lost a tackle or the other team scored a point, he roared, "Grab that hurl with two hands! Get up there and show them who's boss."

A few minutes before half-time, Sam scored a goal against Naas, and the crowd erupted.

Their momentum didn't last long.

At the start of the second half, a Naas forward hit the sliotar over the bar. He scored three more points in quick succession. After the fourth point, Sam's coach smacked his hurley off the goal post. His face turned beetroot red as if he were on the verge of a heart attack.

The woman beside me shook her head. "It's a disgrace, the way he's behaving. Sure, they're only kids."

I couldn't help but laugh.

Kids can play with passion and purpose too.

The ref blew the full-time whistle.

Maynooth: 1−10

Naas: 3−8

Sam's team lost by six points.

The mother turned to me again.

"It's awful. I'll hear all about this in the car on the way home."

"What do you mean?"

"Jonny cried for an hour the last time they lost."

After the match, the coach gathered himself and called the team over.

"You played well today, lads," he said. "You gave it your all. I'm proud."

He prompted them to march across the pitch and shake the other team's hands.

The coach's intense passion was off by a few years, but he also understood every game has winners and losers.

On the way home, I said to Sam, "Sorry about the match. You must be disappointed."

"Yeah," he said. "But, did you see my goal?"

Easter Eggs Ahead

Gamers keep score to unlock new power-ups, compete against themselves or other players, and reach the next level.

There's always another level.

The shy five-year-old who clings to their parent turns into a plucky little eight-year-old or even an ambitious sixteen-year-old. Or perhaps it takes years for them to find their voice and footing. Kids need help from parents, grand-parents, friends, teachers, and even counsellors to progress. But they must still play at school, with their friends, and later in work and in relationships with others.

Kids like to keep score too.

He says, "He got a piece of chocolate, so why can't I?"

And the other:

"She's always allowed to stay up late, but I'm not. That's not fair."

Kids like to deploy the word "fairness" like a Konami Code, so they can get what they want. Parenting is a game dads can play every day too, although best take part for the love of it and not to win. For the first year or two, a dad grinds at the same tasks like changing nappies and cleaning up in the evening time until they can perform them blindfolded.

Tip: to combat boredom, consider multiplayer mode. Involve friends with other kids in suitable plans. It's easier to manage runs to and from football training or early morning matches if the neighbour is going that way with their child too.

Every year, the game of family life offers fresh hurdles to overcome.

I've gotten stuck on particularly difficult challenges while playing: night feeds, temper tantrums, bullies and bullying, school reports, chickenpox, grandparents with competing values, money worries, truculent childminders, sex talks, the Internet, family pets, time or lack thereof.

As soon as I figure out one challenge, a harder one promptly arrives. Unless you count an upset child or partner, I don't get pop-up warnings either, notifying me when I've gone wrong. It's only after the fact that I realise I said "no" or "yes" too quickly or harshly.

When all is lost, I reach for the Konami Code I know best.

Keep going.

Takeaways

Think back to when you were a young teenager. What activities did you enjoy? Did someone show you the way, or did you learn from friends?

Playing games with your kids teaches them a lot about life. You might not like every game your kids wants to play, but that's beside the point. Good ones cover useful traits like teamwork, grit and losing with grace. They also serve as a healthy outlet for physical or creative energy.

Kids learn from playing games with their friends and other groups too. Perhaps it's a video game, like *Mario Kart* on Nintendo, a team sports game like football at the weekend, or a board game over the holidays.

Learning how to keep score, when to play to win and just for fun will help you and your children break through to the next level.

Konami Code Tips

- Expecting your kids to pursue the same interests that captivated your attention when you were their age is a recipe for disappointment. Best find new common ground.
- Enrol them in team sports as soon as they're old enough. Finding the right activity might take a few tries, but games are a great avenue for burning off excess energy.
- If you're playing against your child, let him or her win every now and again, especially when they're younger; it'll give them the confidence to keep practising.
- On the flip side, teach your child how to win and lose with grace through your actions.

TWENTY
LET IT GO

She's so small.
After the school bell rings,
Alone on a wooden chair.

———

Starting school for the first time is a big day for any child. It's a big day for their parents too.

On the morning of Maria's first day of primary school, Audrey combed her hair into plaits and helped her put on a pressed pinafore, white shirt and tie.

Maria's small hands fumbled with the small buttons.

"I can't do them. I don't know how."

"I'll show you," said Audrey.

While she helped Maria dress, I cooked sausages and scrambled eggs. Sam, who was also starting back at school, got little attention that morning.

"Hurry up, you're going to be late," I shouted up the stairs in between burning the sausages and overcooking the eggs.

"I'm so excited," said Maria. Her cheeks were bright red from scrubbing her face.

"School is fun," I said.

"Is it?"

Most of the time.

After breakfast, she messed around with a *Frozen* Play-Doh set an aunt bought her for her birthday a few days beforehand.

"Don't get your clothes dirty!" said Audrey.

Maria's grandmother called to see her off and take pictures of us at the front door.

"You can leave your coat behind today," said Audrey. "It's warm outside."

Maria put on an enormous pink and mostly empty school bag, with a picture of Olaf on the back. The primary school was only a few hundred metres from our house, so my wife and I walked with Maria to her classroom.

Some of her new classmates, the well-behaved ones, were already sitting at their desks, shining in their pressed new uniforms with copybooks and colouring pencils in front of them.

The classroom and hall outside were full of helpless parents, some fighting back the tears and afraid to let their son or daughter go.

The teacher Clíona spent as much time reassuring the boys and girls as talking to the anxious parents and walking them towards the door.

"They'll be fine, they'll be fine. It's best if you go."

Maria clung to Audrey's leg.

"Come on, I'll help you sit down, Maria," she said, pulling Maria's fingers off her jeans. "You'll love school."

With much coaxing, Maria agreed to sit on the small wooden chair, albeit clinging onto the cold, yellow handles of her seat.

"Don't worry, school is fun," I said, pushing a strand of hair from her shoulder. "You'll see."

"I'm not sure," she said in a small voice. "Don't go."

Audrey hugged her.

As we left, Maria looked at us with large, helpless blue eyes.

"Bye," she whispered.

"She's in the system now," I said to my wife on the way back to the house. Upstairs in the home office, I logged into a work conference call. But I couldn't concentrate.

A new baby doesn't want to let go of their mother; they're still intimately connected. A parent can't let a toddler out of their sight for more than a few minutes in case they stick a finger in the plug socket, pull a glass out of the press or even fall down the stairs. But once they start school, it's a parent's job to step back. Some days that job is straightforward; some days, it's hard.

A few months before starting school, we'd taught Maria how to hold a fork properly while still tucking her in at night. Like many parents, it was perplexing to find ourselves caught between her early childhood and this new wider world.

Now we'd sent her into a system that demanded we play the role of bystanders for large chunks of the week. One day she will emerge the other side shaped by experiences outside of our control, and stare up into the real world, almost an adult.

One friend who teaches primary school kids told us,

new starters often confess things like, "I think I love you more than my Mammy." She also grumbled some kids arrive at school hopelessly unprepared. "I spend hours the first few weeks helping them take off their coats, sit down and go to the bathroom."

Although Maria was shy during her first few weeks at school, she was an altogether different child at home. Her favourite film was Disney's *Frozen*, and she liked nothing more than standing in front of the television and singing the theme song *Let It Go*.

I enjoyed listening to Maria sing the first half a dozen times, and we shared the obligatory videos with family.

While she sang, I lay on the couch worrying about grown-up stuff like how to improve my running times, going bald and if it was my turn to put out the bins.

Meanwhile, Maria played the song over and over.

I couldn't hold it back any more.

"Do we have to listen to that again?"

"You don't like *Frozen*?"

"I do, but we listen to it every day. Why do you like *Frozen* so much, anyway?"

"I like Olaf because he's made of snow."

Like many parents, I complained about the way Kristen Anderson-Lopez's song lodged its way into the back of my skull.

"I swear, when I close my eyes, I can hear that bloody song on repeat. I want one day in my life without Kristen bloody Anderson-Lopez, Olaf and magical princesses." I complained to Mary, a friend from work. "Disney is shipping a lie. Real life isn't about princes and princesses."

"You're turning into a crank. Have you even watched the film? Disney is progressive now," she said.

When we asked Maria about school that first year, she said little most days beyond, "It's OK."

During our first parent-teacher meeting, her teacher told us Maria is "quite shy".

But at home, Maria thought of little else but *Frozen*. With our help, she covered her bedroom walls with posters of Anna, Elsa and Olaf. Her bookshelf sagged with *Frozen* annuals and stories. Her aunt even bought a coveted and overpriced *Frozen* doll as a Christmas present.

Maria clapped her hands together after opening the box. "Princess Anna!"

Who Else Wants More Olaf In Their Life?

A few years later. New teachers. New friends. New music. Different problems.

Maria replaced *Let It Go* with a pop song by George Ezra, a British pop singer with a voice like gravel. She ran for class rep and gathered a collection of friends I could barely keep track of. Audrey put the princess dresses, now too small, into a plastic bag in our attic.

One morning while getting Maria's uniform out for school, I found the Princess Anna doll stuffed at the back of the wardrobe.

"Why do you like George Ezra so much?" I said to her after she played his song *Shotgun* for the fifth time in the car.

"You don't understand, Dad."

"Try me."

"It's just a good song. I can sing the words."

"We know."

"I want to go see him play. Can I?"

"I'm not promising anything."

That November, Disney released a trailer for a new *Frozen* film. Anna, Elsa and Olaf were coming back... and this time to a cinema near us.

I can handle a little more Kristen Anderson-Lopez in my life. I'm ready. All is forgiven Disney.

I checked the cinema timetable – disaster. The trailer turned out to be a teaser for an animated short about Olaf, hardly worth the effort of a cinema trip. Disney pushed the release of *Frozen II* back until 2019. I understood the film-makers' desire to create a worthy sequel, but a six-year gap between releases represented almost the entirety of my daughter's early childhood years.

When they finally released it, Maria told me: "Yeah, I dunno about that one, Dad. I really want to go and see *Trolls*."

I cared little for *Trolls*. So, I pressed her on such fickle loyalties. She put down the Nintendo Switch, stood up straight, hands on her hips.

"Dad, don't you know I'm too big for *Frozen* now? I don't even wear princess dresses anymore. It's not what I want."

"I can get the dresses out of the attic if you like?"

"You're crazy."

Press Pause Please

Sometimes we get what we want.

Disney's shareholders got a sequel that earned far more at the box office than its predecessor, ensuring the franchise has at least another five years of life. The same year Disney released *Frozen II*, Audrey took Maria to watch George Ezra play at Malahide Castle in Dublin.

I got some of what I want too.

I can't remember the last time I've listened to *Let It Go* or even *Shotgun*, although both lyrics still trigger reflex memories.

I hired a long-distance running coach to help me train, and I outsourced leaving out the bins to Sam. I even bought special thickening shampoo for my hair (the verdict is still out). But what I need is a giant pause button. Walking Maria to school on a warm autumn morning, an oversized pink bag on her small back, seems like yesterday. To her, it's a fading dream.

A mental snapshot of a little girl who'd just mastered the art of using a fork, shining in a pressed red pinafore calling out "don't go" isn't enough.

I can't do anything about the passage of time. No parent can. Instead, it's onto the next thing. And the next.

Takeaways

The first few years with small kids pass by like an intense rush, in part because free time is such a rare commodity. One day you'll look up and wonder when did they get so tall and how did the years pass so fast?

Starting school is a particularly big landmark for kids, mams and even dads. It's their first step into the wider world and the moment when you regain some potential free time. Instead of holding onto the good times (or the bad ones), settle in for what's next.

With family, something new is always imminent. When in doubt, frame it like this:

Zero to one year: A parent lives life in blocks of four hours until the baby sleeps through the night.

One to five years: Full of energy, they need the most hands-on care and attention.

Five to nine years: Still innocent, they're unlikely to start drinking dishwasher rinse aid from the kitchen shelf.

Nine to twelve years: The years before becoming teenagers, they begin forming a new sense of self beyond the family unit.

Thirteen to eighteen years: The teenage years. Best not to treat them like kids anymore.

Tips for School Starters

- Book the morning off work to take pictures and bring them to school. It's a small but important family milestone, and one you can't repeat.
- Expect them to return from school tired and short on answers about their day until they settle in.

TWENTY-ONE

HAIR

Floppy fringe,
Cheeky chop.
Oh, what did I do?

Baby style is a lot like adult style. How you dress your kids says as much about you as them.

This fringe won't work.

Aged fourteen and back from the barbers, I inspected the results of my haircut in the bathroom mirror.

I know, I'll fix it myself.

I took a small nail scissors from the press and trimmed my fringe. I snipped one side closer than the other and took an inch off my fringe.

Disaster!

The bathroom was all out of hair clippers. In my

teenage wisdom, I grabbed an old Gillette disposable razor and shaved the tuft of my scalp.

But, I went against the grain and cut into my fringe. When the blood dripped down my forehead and into the sink, I knew I'd gone too far.

I could get away with wearing a baseball cap around the house and the street, but how would I negotiate school?

The next morning, I snuck into morning assembly and stood at the back, pressing the palm of my hand against my butchered forehead.

"What's wrong with you?" whispered Daire.

"Oh, nothing, I have a headache."

I was confident about the rest of the day until I got to Maths class. Mr Murphy, who had a thick ginger mane and beard to match, asked me a question about quadratic equations.

I looked down at my book and mumbled an answer, a hand pressed over my forehead.

"Mr Collins, remove your hand from your forehead when I'm talking to you."

"But sir—"

"Immediately, Mr Collins!"

I lowered my hand, and the class erupted. Mr Murphy laughed until he was red in the face.

"My God, Mr Collins!"

When I finally got out of Maths class, dozens of students were waiting outside to glimpse my self-inflicted hair calamity.

I shrugged my shoulders as if to say, *What can you do?*

Our school enforced a strict uniform policy, so a hair-style was our only means of liberation.

We stood around the lunch hall with Dax Wax and Brylcreem practically dripping off our fringes. Some lads bleached their hair a bright shade of orange. Others grew their hair down to their shoulders. Only a few shaved their heads, but none with a disposable razor like me.

Growing older, I experimented with different styles, combing my hair straight up, spiking it and splitting it down the middle. In my early twenties, I settled on an enormous quiff held aloft with Dax Wax, kind of like Ross from the US sitcom *Friends*.

One night in college, a girl said to me, "No girl would want to run their hands through that grease ball!"

I spent hours in the supermarket the next morning, agonising over the right type of hair product.

"Can I help you, sir?" an attendant asked.

"I need a better product, something that will take the fluffy look out of my hair but which I can still wash out."

"Have you tried Brylcreem?"

"I've tried them all."

Gel. Wax. Clay. Putty. Hair spray.

I thought I had ninety-nine hair problems. It turned out I had just one.

In my early twenties, I mistakenly believed I'd inherited my dad's crop of thick bushy hair.

"Baldness won't happen to me," I told my friends.

Over the next few years, I discovered I'd inherited my hairline from my mam's side. Her father was as bald as a snooker cue.

Mine started thinning after Sam was born. I'm not quite bald yet, but my hair is spray painted with grey, the ridge of my skull threatening to erupt between what's left of my crown. Even today, strands of hair grow out from the spot where I shaved against the grain in an odd direction to the rest of my fringe.

Not that it matters.

The older I get, the less hair I have. And the expensive shampoos? They do nothing.

I enjoy commiserating with other follicle-challenged dads. Most of them have little hair to comb or style either.

More than a few friends can trace the path of their receding hairlines back to the moment a doctor announced, "It's a boy!" or "It's a girl!"

"It's because of the stress of the kids," I remind them.

They nod solemnly, their shining domes sparkling under the bar lights.

So, I live vicariously through my kids' hairstyles.

A few years ago, Audrey tasked me with getting my daughter ready for school each morning, as she'd to leave for work early. The first few mornings didn't go well.

"Ow! You're hurting me!" Maria complained. Aged five, she was wise to the fact that no, dads don't know everything.

"I need to get these knots out," I said, tugging on the bottom of a particularly difficult strand of hair.

"Stop it, Dad!"

"It's not my fault girls don't come with an instruction manual."

We found a way around the problem with a special type of dad-proof brush: the Tangle Teezer. A lightweight plastic instrument, it glided through her knots and curls like a warmed-up runner three miles into an easy run.

Combing through knots without tears is a lucrative business. Last time I checked, Tangle Teezer inventor Shaun Pulfrey is worth $15 million.

After much instruction and practice, we settled on a single style I could manage in five minutes: pigtails.

I thought I was pretty good at pigtails, but my daughter still reminds me, "You were terrible. They fell out all the time in school."

These days, when I question her latest look in the morning, she rolls her eyes.

"You don't know style."

It's a Ronnie!

"What's that on your chin?" Sam's aunt asked. "Are you growing something out?"

"I want to see if I can grow a moustache," said Sam, now fourteen. He rubbed the dark shadow under his nose and gazed wistfully into the distance.

"A what?!" said his aunt.

"A moustache," said Sam.

"I can't believe I have a son with a Ronnie," said Audrey.[1]

I had flashbacks of shaving my fringe. So, I gave Sam my spare electric razor and explained how all the buttons work.

I brought him up to the bathroom, ran the razor over the grey hairs of my beard.

"Always shave with the grain," I said. "Anything else, it'll turn into a nasty rash."

Then, I showed him how to use a razor blade to trim a Ronnie.

Sam was about the same age as I was when hair gel became an object of obsession for us in school.

Sam and some of his friends have a tenacity for sprouting tufts of hair on their chins and upper lips. But, they care little for Dax Wax, Brylcreem, clay and spray.

The Generation Z males, or the Zoomers, around these parts insist on the fade. This expensive haircut takes at least half an hour and lasts all of three weeks if you're lucky.

Sam's variation involved shaving the sides of his hair skin-tight, growing a fringe down to his nose and blowing drying the results. I awake most mornings to the sound of his hair drier on max power.

"You'll have to start paying for your own haircuts," I told him. "I can't keep you in fades."

"A haircut is a human right..."

"Human rights only go so far in this house!"

When Sam and a group of his friends are together, I can't tell who is who. They stand around street corners in black puffer jackets, their immaculately blow-dried fringes growing past their eyeballs: clothes and hairstyles hallmarks of their tribe.

At least you could see our faces when we were his age.

I looked up an old school friend online recently. A great man for hair gel back in the day, I was pleased to see he was still sporting the same spiky, greasy style some twenty years later. I value consistency. I also value seeing someone's forehead.

"Did you ever consider hair gel?" I said to Sam.

"Nah."

"You're better off," I told him. "Those products will turn you bald."

"You're just jealous because you've no hair."

"Enjoy it while it lasts. Your grandfather on your mother's side was completely bald. Everyone knows that's where hairlines come from. You can't fight genetics."

"Is that what happened to you?"

"No," I said. "You did."

He's Got Baby Style

K was born with a severe case of cradle cap. It took a few months to shift. Audrey thinks it's because she bought a special ointment for babies at the pharmacy and applied it morning and night.

I know it's because I flattened his curly hair in the bath with warm water, blow-dried and styled it in unusual directions.

These days, when I try to comb his hair, he grips my beard with his small hands and laughs. Depending on my mood and what I ate for dinner, I'll brush his hair upwards, backwards or to the side. I like recreating my styles of old.

Not that it matters.

As soon as I'm done, he runs his small hands through his hair, messing up my hard work, and runs off down the stairs calling "mam!"

I'm one step away from shopping for baby Dax Wax and Brylcreem. I might not get another chance.

Early one school morning, Maria appeared at the bottom of the stairs groomed, pressed and shining, as if to say ta-da!

"What do you think of my plaits?" she said. "I did them myself."

"I prefer pigtails."

"You don't know style."

"I know baby style."

I was surprised to see her up and ready so early as I usually spend twenty minutes calling to get up out of bed or, "You'll miss your bus."

After breakfast, she knelt down to say goodbye to K. He grinned, reached out, wrapped his hands around her neck and clasped her plaits with both hands.

"Oww!" she said. "You're not to do that."

He laughed and locked his finger into her hair like a vice. His fingers turned white.

"Make him stop, Dad. Do something!"

I reached for his fingers.

"Let go K, you're hurting your sister."

I tried to tell him, I really did. But he wouldn't listen. You can protest, fight and struggle, but some days love won't let you go.

Takeaways

Dad pants. Dad shirts. Dad bods. Guys with kids face a lot of clichés about how they look. Some older guys dress in clothes that are relics from when they first became a dad years ago. It's as if the gods of fashion froze time when a new dad's partner announced, "I'm pregnant."

Ripped bootcut jeans, cargo pants and plaid shirts, I've been there. I still am some days. Guys like me prefer shopping in bulk for clothes once or twice a year. It's more economical and efficient.

Dads don't need Giorgio Armani's sense of style, but ensuring they look presentable in the morning before school, a trip to their friends or their grandparents is part of the job. And it helps if we scrub up too. Otherwise, we'll frighten their friends' parents.

Mothers style their babies based on what they like and enjoy it. Instead of fighting baby fashion, have fun with it.

Audrey doesn't like ironing, and it bothered me to watch Sam go off to school in a wrinkled shirt. So, I started ironing his shirt on Sunday evenings.

If you have a son, expect people to comment on how you both look alike if the pair of you arrive in matching jeans or shirts. If you've a daughter, expect to spend time learning skills like the ins and outs of pigtails, hairclips and dresses, *assuming* that's what she likes. She might prefer cropping her hair, in which case you're off the hook.

Kids' interests form as much from their personalities as from anything their parents believe they like.

Growing kids and teenagers like expressing their identities through clothes, hairstyles and hallmarks of their particular tribe.

Have fun with that too. Remember, becoming a dad is about more than providing. Take care of your kids so they feel good about themselves.

Babystyle Tips

- Got girls with long hair in your life? Invest in a Tangle Teezer or similar hairbrush. It'll prevent tears and simplify your mornings.
- When your son wants to learn how to shave, show him even if he's not quite ready. Otherwise, he could go against the grain with a rusty razor.

TWENTY-TWO

DREAM COUNTRY

Reading from our book,
Sounding words, safe in our nook,
An ending leaves me shook.

Teaching kids how to read offers a chance to relax together for a few minutes at the end of a busy day. This one-on-one window closes quickly.

"What books do you read, Dad?" said Maria one night when she was five.

"That's a hard question," I said.

"Tell me."

Audrey and I bought her different pictures books for Christmas and birthdays. Reading books like these to a baby or toddler is easy. Plus, it expands a child's vocabulary faster than any zany YouTuber.

They sit on your lap, flicking through a colourful hard-back and point at the pictures of cows, dogs and sheep for all of 120 seconds.

"That's a cat. That's a dog. That's a cow. And what does the cow say?"

"Moooo."

"Well done!"

Cue thunderous cheers and applause.

"No, don't try and rip the pages."

After a few minutes, they'll either jump down and find something else to do or pick up a second book for you to read.

A couple of words at a time is more than enough for babies. A couple of books at a time is seldom enough for me.

Usually, I devour biographies, business and self-help books. I'm hungry for advice and strategies to apply at work or in my business. I keep three titles on the go: a Kindle, paperback, and an audiobook that I listen to on times-two playback speed.

I read the books early in the morning or late at night, and I listen to audiobooks while out for long walks or slow runs. If information is currency, I've tried to become rich.

I'm not there yet, though.

Reading these non-fiction books isn't enough. I take the good ones apart, outlining and mind-mapping lessons from engaging titles and abandoning the rest.

I keep a list of book-reading rules too. Put a boring one down after fifty pages. Read outside of my comfort zone. Try non-fiction in the morning and fiction late at night.

When I'm on holidays or have more time off, I read novels for pleasure. On a normal week, my patience for fiction, much less tales of giants and Dream Country, is depressingly short.

"What books do you read, Dad?"

"Books about other people in the news," I said.

A five-year-old has little interest in the story of Nike's founder Phil Knight and how he solved his company's supply chain issues, in Steve Jobs's attempts to put a ding in the universe, or why Elon Musk wants to go to Mars.

"That sounds boring, Dad. What books did you read when you were little?" she said.

"*The BFG* was a good one."

"Can we read that?"

Big Words

I considered reading *The BFG* to Maria using a tablet, but they presented too many distractions for both of us. All those YouTube videos were only a notification and a click away.

I found a used paperback of *The BFG*, one with an orange and yellow cover and illustrations from Quentin Blake, on my bookshelf. A book without Internet access, YouTuber notifications, or unfinished to-do lists.

One night, I helped Maria get ready for bed, prompted her to wash her teeth and then produced the book.

"Yaaay," she said.

The BFG is a terrifying yet funny story about a young British orphan and a big friendly giant. The BFG kidnaps Sophie from her bed and whisks her away to Dream Country, a land populated by even larger giants who eat small children.

A fine tale, yes, but reading *The BFG* aloud to Maria was harder than expected. It was an exercise in learning how to slow down, and not one I set out to relearn either.

At first, I tried to read *The BFG to* Maria like she was

still a toddler. I sat on the edge of her bed at night and rushed through the first few pages of the book.

"Slow down, Daddy. You're going too fast. I want to hear about Sophie's school. All these words are so big."

"I know."

It took several nights to learn about Sophie's school, the first chapter in the book.

The BFG is full of dozens of pages with multi-syllable words to negotiate together.

Each night, Maria stopped me to ask questions like:

"Why is the BFG so tall?"

"Do giants really eat small children?"

And:

"What's a 'whizzpopper'?"

(That's the BFG's word for flatulence.)

Maria wanted to tackle sounding out bigger multi-syllable words like "mountain" and "Dream Country" and "horse feathers".

"I want to show my teacher."

We sat around sounding out syllable by syllable, and all the while, I wondered if I was falling behind at work.

Why did Steve Jobs buy Pixar in the first place? And would Elon Musk ever rescue Tesla? And how was I going to pay myself and all those contractors I'd hired this month?

We spent a few months with *The BFG*. We'd read one chapter and then return to the previous one to fill in what she understood about *The BFG*, Sophie and Giant Country. More than once, she caught me jumping ahead. The tattered book became a portal into my childhood.

"You skipped a bit, Dad. Let's go back."

Some nights, we spent more time going backwards than forwards, an act more like a painting than reading.

I don't remember reaching The End together, but one

fine spring evening, Maria met me in the hall in her purple pyjamas. She held a tattered, dog-eared copy of *The BFG* in the air.

"We finished!"

"We did? I don't believe it."

She flicked to the last page.

"Look."

The two of us high-fived the end of Dream Country.

Lights Out

I bought Maria some of Dahl's other books like *Fantastic Mister Fox* and *James and the Giant Peach*. I even fished a tattered yellow copy of *Mathilda* from a cardboard box at the back of our attic that I'd read as a teenager.

Finishing *The BFG* gave Maria newfound confidence to tackle books on her own. I brought her down to Easons and our local bookstore, where she asked the sales assistant for books by David Walliams and Jacqueline Wilson.

Although I could technically read them aloud, too, these were stories she found rather than ones I presented to her.

Aged seven, she sat up straight in bed, the way only a small child can before they learn to hunch over their work and worries, surrounded by Beanie Boo teddy bears, whispering sentence after sentence.

"This is Tom. He is twelve and goes to a posh boarding school."

That's from *The Midnight Gang* by David Walliams.

"This story starts with a dress."

That's *Rent a Bridesmaid* by Jacqueline Wilson.

"Most people look forward to the holidays, but the stretch between Thanksgiving and Christmas just makes me a nervous wreck."

That's *Diary of a Wimpy Kid: Cabin Fever* by Jeff Kinney.

Putting Maria to bed didn't take as long anymore. She set aside the teddy bears and picked up a paperback. Instead of reading entire sentences aloud, she sounded out the occasional troublesome word.

I stood at the door, listening to her vocabulary expand, and her attention span grow. I envied her lack of self-consciousness, her capacity for immersion in another world.

It's harder for an adult to climb down the rabbit hole with the same sense of wonder and awe.

I returned to Elon Musk, Steve Jobs and Phil Knight. I'd picked back up my to-do list. I'd even more free time to grind down the remains of my attention span with my iPhone.

My nights weren't entirely free.

One night, I was listening to ambient music over noise-cancelling headphones so I could focus on editing a free-lance article. She tapped me on the shoulder, and I jumped out of the chair.

"You gave me a fright!"

"Dad," she said, holding a book in her hand. "Board-ing school, what's a boarding school?"

"It's kind of like Sophie's school in the BFG."

"Oooh, a boarding school, I get it. I'm glad I don't go to one of those."

"We certainly thought about it!"

As the year passed, her questions became less frequent. Five minutes of reading alone before an intervention from a supposedly more literate parent turned into ten... then twenty.

Until finally, I told her, "Lights out, please, put the book away and go to sleep, you've school tomorrow."

"Daaaad, I'm not even tired."

"Come on."

"One more page?"

"You won't be able to function tomorrow."

"I will, I promise."

One frosty Tuesday morning, Maria got up before me. She dressed, brushed her hair and toasted some waffles for breakfast.

"You're up early?"

"I don't want to miss my bus."

While I was brewing coffee, she packed her lunch and put on her red coat, school bag and scarf.

"I'm off to school, Dad."

She kissed me on the cheek goodbye and walked down to the bus stop.

After she left, I went upstairs to her bedroom to find she'd made her bed and tidied her clothes away. On her desk lay a stack of half-a-dozen dogeared books by Roald Dahl, Jacqueline Wilson and Dav Pilkey.

It was quite the pile.

Pride rose up in my chest that she could finish these books without asking me many questions or losing interest. I marvelled at her rapidly growing attention span. Perhaps it'd surpass my own?

Then, I saw the books for what they were. Markers for the fresh ways Maria didn't need me as much anymore. And that stack would only grow.

Takeaways

If you want to teach your kids a skill, do it first. For example, pointing out pictures in a "brand new book". Then do it with them. For example, sounding out the words together.

Next, encourage them to try without your help. Finally, enable them to do it themselves by letting them buy books of their choosing.

Kids enjoy reading more if they see their parents with a book in their hands. Buy them books for their age group and also one or two more advanced titles. Leave them where they play to pick up and browse, except for paperbacks. Toddlers love ripping up those!

Creating an evening routine around reading works well. You could, for example, spend a few minutes reading several pages from a short book to your son or daughter before bedtime.

When they're small, you don't even have to finish the story either. Babies don't care what you read to them as long as they're up on your lap listening to the sound of your voice and looking at colourful pictures.

With toddlers, a few pages a night is more than enough to hold their attention span and spark their imagination.

With older kids, either take them to the bookshop with an "unlimited book-buying budget" or the local library. When they finish one book, reward them with another.

Keep it up, and one day, your son or daughter will read a book of their choosing without your help. That's a heart-breaking goal for every dad.

Tips for Wannabe Bookworms

- Create a book-buying rule. "If they want it, get it." Kids toys are expensive, especially anything small, imported and plastic. Books, on the other hand, offer greater rewards than anything you can earn from cash deposited in the bank. Plus, you'll probably save money down the road on extra tuition.

- If you have an older son or daughter who says they don't like reading, buy them audiobooks instead. Pay no attention to those who claim listening to audiobooks isn't reading. It's a great way of enjoying a book without feeling like it's work.

PART THREE
GROWING UP

Uncle Ben: "Peter, look. You're changing. I know. I went through exactly the same thing at your age."

Peter Parker: "No. Not exactly."

TWENTY-THREE

SEX TALK

I'm filling the gaps
in what you know, coming next:
Respect and protect.

---

*The big talk isn't a one-off deal, but it's best not to wait too
long to initiate it.*

"Did you do your homework?" I asked Sam one night at
dinner.

"Balls!" He slapped his head and laughed.

A few days later, he started dropping words like "boobs"
into casual conversation, and if a couple kissed on television
and worked their way to the bedroom, Sam covered his
mouth and sniggered.

If a sex scene appeared on TV, I followed my dad's

approach: I changed the channel as fast as possible. But that was little more than a plaster.

I put off telling my nine-year-old son the facts about sex for too long. He picked up worrying snippets of information from friends, television and even some video games and began assembling them like a monstrous puzzle. Friends and relations with kids told me Sam needed someone to draw it all together for him.

The big talk held all the appeal of standing on a rusty nail.

Before my parents broached sex with me while growing up, I'd already picked up most of the facts from a biology book a friend shared with me beforehand.

My parents sat my brother and me down on the couch one evening and explained as if we knew nothing. We must have asked a few hard questions because halfway through, my dad said:

"Can you both go upstairs? Your mother and I need to talk."

I heard loud voices coming from the sitting room for a bit.

Half an hour later, they called us back down and restarted the sex talk. It was like wandering around an awkward maze.

Still, Sam had an idea about sex, and my job was to fill in these gaps.

I waited until a trip to Disney World in Florida that summer. We spent the first few days enjoying the rides.

Magic Kingdom didn't feel like the right place to get into why his body was sprouting hair and where babies come from, what with Mickey Mouse, Olaf, Princess Elsa and the cast of *Frozen* marching past us towards the Animal Kingdom.

So I waited a few days until the kids had their fill of parades, rides, and Disney World.

"Sam, we're going on a day trip to NASA," I announced over pancakes and maple syrup one morning. "That's where they went to the moon, and if you're lucky, you'll get to see a space rocket."

"I don't want to go," he said. "Who has time for space rockets? It sounds boring."

"Who doesn't like space rockets? Your teacher will be delighted when she hears you're learning so much. Think of it as like a science field trip."

If I were a more honest man, I'd have swapped the word science for biology.

"You're going," said his mother, more enthused by the prospects of an all-day break from the two of us than my plans to explain how an egg is fertilised.

It took some convincing, but a nine-year-old's odds are slight in the face of united parents. An hour later, my reluctant son and I set out in our rented Ford Escape from Orlando towards Cape Canaveral.

We drove in silence until I got the hang of roads. After about half an hour, I tried small talk as a warm-up to the main event.

"Do you miss school?"

"No."

"What about your friends? You must miss Conal. He's a good chap."

He was also the type of chap who delighted in calling up to our house, peeing all over the toilet seat and never flushing – the things we put up with for the love of our children.

"Yeah, maybe."

"What about the girls? Do you miss any of them?"

"God, no, why would I miss them? Girls are awful."

"Sometimes when a boy becomes..."

And we were off. It might seem weird to broach sex while on a road trip to NASA.

Perhaps it's an Irish thing. Most men I know don't consciously meet up to talk about what's on their mind over coffee or a playdate. Instead, we approach problems and decisions sideways. The golf courses of Ireland are like a therapist's room for repressed men. Or you hike up a small mountain, like Croagh Patrick, and a friend confesses he wants to propose to his girlfriend, but she doesn't want kids.

We approach problems and big-life decisions sideways. Talking about problem head-on, for the Irish men I know, is like staring into the sun.

A long car journey meant I'd have a captive audience for an hour or two, more than enough time to cover the basics.

"I hear Conal's Mam had a baby recently. Did he tell you much about it?"

"No, why would he?"

"Take out your headphones. I've something to say..."

I explained the mechanics of how sex worked, taking care to stick to medical terms like penis, vagina and fertilising the egg.

"It's not polite to going around using words like boobs and balls over dinner."

He laughed.

"That's what I'm talking about!"

I offered a few additional insights I'd lifted from a parenting book and rehearsed with my wife and friends in the pub a few weeks before our trip.

"Sex is something men and women do to have babies or for fun," I said to him. "But it's for adults."

I paused for a minute.

"And sometimes men and men have sex or women and women have sex and... well, it's for adults, that's what you need to know."

"Men and men?" he said.

"Yes, gay people enjoy making love as well, like the couple who lived a few doors up from us."

His eyes widened. I was on unsure footing. Who was I to bring the neighbours into it?

Google Maps lit up.

"Your destination is on the right."

Where's My Map?

Kennedy Space Center looked like a cardboard box from Christmas day blown 526 feet into the sky and painted with the American flag and NASA logo.

Unfortunately, we were a few days early.

"We're in the middle of preparing for a launch," said the Kennedy Space centre attendant. "SpaceX is sending a satellite into space. You should come back next weekend and watch it."

"Can we, Dad?"

"We would if we weren't flying home on Friday."

My timing, much like with the sex talk, was off.

Instead, we opted for the next best thing: a guided tour of Kennedy Space Center.

Inside the station, the space shuttle *Atlantis* hung from the ceiling, rotated to the side, its payload open, all of its parts on display.

I asked my son to take a picture of the shuttle with his iPhone.

"This is what the future looks like," I said, standing

underneath the shuttle. "Or perhaps what we thought it would look like twenty years ago."

"Look at this awesome space toilet, Dad," he said. "I can't find the button. How do they flush it?"

He sat on the toilet and pulled on a tube overhead.

"I wouldn't touch that," I said. "Anything could happen."

Later on, we learnt about NASA's mission to land on Mars and how it will involve multi-year trips between now and 2030.

"They're going; they're actually going," I said.

During the drive back, I was confident enough to recover old ground. Like any productive field trip, a little repetition would ensure we both learnt something useful.

"So, do you have any questions about what I said earlier..."

"The space toilet?"

"Sex and where babies come from, how they're made, adult relationships..."

"Yeah, I get it now, Dad. It's kind of like when I'm playing *Grand Theft Auto.*"

"Grand Theft what?"

"I was playing it at my uncle's house ages ago, and there–"

"You're not allowed to play GTA!"

"–And there was a strip club in the game, I went in for a minute, and there were all these boobs, but then I turned the Playstation off. What is a strip club, anyway?"

They hadn't covered this topic in the parenting book I'd read on the plane.

"A strip club is where adults dance without clothes."

"Why would they dance without clothes?"

"Because... because adults do things differently than

boys your age. I wouldn't worry too much about it until you're older."

"How old?"

"How about never?"

I was prying on the outer edges of his knowledge of sex.

"But don't play that game again! And boobs isn't the right word to use either. They're called breasts."

My son picked up his iPhone, and I drove in silence for a few minutes. My answer wasn't good enough, but my dwindling control over his digital life was a bigger issue. It was also a problem that would only escalate as he grew older.

Before travelling to the States, I'd mentioned it in passing to my mother.

"We didn't have the Internet when you were a child," she said.

"That's no help."

"You could buy him a book?"

"He doesn't like reading."

An hour outside of Cape Canaveral, I tried again.

"You might come across a picture or a video of adults having sex. It's called porn and isn't real life," I said. "It's... it's something adults make or watch for fun."

"Something weird came up on my phone the other day," he said. "I closed straight out of it."

"That's... I'm glad you told me."

I left myself a mental note to recheck his phone when we got back to the rented house.

His grandmother bought the phone for him the previous December. I'd never installed parental monitoring software, although I insisted I could hack into his device and check it from my computer. The lies we tell our children.

"But you know where babies come from now?" I said.

Sam looked out the car window at a sports car over-taking us.

"Ah yeah, sure, we heard about that one in school months ago," he said. "Wait, was that a Lambo?"

"What did you say?"

"Daaaad."

That night at dinner, my wife asked about the talk.

I told her about the strip club.

"Oh God, it sounds so awkward. I don't want to hear anymore."

(A year or two later, when Audrey was pregnant with K, she used this opportunity to begin the sex talk with Maria.)

Face Facts

At home in Ireland a few weeks later, I told a few friends with kids about the sex talk.

"We covered the essentials," I said, feeling rather proud of myself. "I'm glad it's all over, and I never have to go through that again."

"But you know you're not done, right?" my friend said.

"I know a few questions might come up during puberty and..."

"Did you cover changes to his body and what he can expect and how he should behave?" said my wife.

Crap.

I'd missed those items on my sex talk to-do list.

"It never really ends," said my friend. "You have to keep talking to them until they *get it*."

Until they get it.

How would I know when I've reached that point? Would I get a notification like on a Google Maps journey?

We were fumbling towards adulthood. It's one thing to know the facts of life, but it's quite another to understand it. Talking to kids about sex, however uncomfortable, isn't a one-time deal.

A few weeks later, I took Sam to see the new *Avengers* movie. During the drive to the cinema, I got into the sex talk 2.0.

"Some of your friends will have girlfriends, and some will have boyfriends. Whatever your preferences, that's OK once you respect other people's choices."

"I will, Dad."

"Some people won't. Ignore them."

A few months later, Audrey became pregnant with K. It was a nice little talking point for the next part of our ongoing conversation.

"Yes, Sam, parents still have sex. Contraception matters, and we can cover it later when you're older."

"Dad, Jesus. I don't need to know this."

"But you do! And don't worry," I said. "He's the last baby for our family."

"Are we nearly at the cinema? It's starting soon."

I pulled up at a busy roundabout, and the traffic lights turned red. Dozens of cars chugged past us. I looked at my son and then at the time.

"Well?"

"It's taking longer than I expected."

Our short road trip is now a multi-year expedition.

Takeaways

Start early. By the time you talk to your kids about the facts of life, they'll have already picked up an alarming amount of information from their friends, television and the Internet.

Kids learn fast, so it's not always easy to control their information sources. Although they may already know the basics, they probably will have big gaps in their knowledge. It's your job to fill them.

Talking to older kids about sex and the facts of life isn't a one-off conversation. It's a recurring topic as they transition from young teen to young adult. Your ongoing chats reduce risky behaviours and build their self-esteem, plus they keep you up-to-date on growing trends.

It's also a good idea to let your curious teen know they can confide without fear of repercussions.

Facts of Life Tips

- If, like me, you're uncomfortable about the big talk, rehearse it beforehand with your partner or a friend with kids and iron out any kinks.
- Buy a modern facts-of-life book for your son or daughter. Television shows and movies also suffice. They serve as good conversation starters, i.e. "Did you read that book I bought you yet?"
- Consider broaching the sex talk while engaged in another activity, like out for a drive. Asking them to sit down, close the door and listen can feel overwhelming.
- Use the correct anatomical names for body parts. It will prevent stigma and laughing about odd words.

TWENTY-FOUR

MONEY

Statement's evidence:
Netflix, Amazon, takeout
Stop spending, son!

Talking to a son or daughter about money is a rewarding experience for both parties.

At least a half-million euros.

That's how much it costs to raise two children from birth to twenty-four years[1] in Ireland, assuming a parent isn't contributing thousands extra to their new home, a wedding or bailing them out of a foreign holiday gone awry.

Ireland is also lucky enough to claim affordable healthcare and education for most. Both systems are far from perfect, but those lucky enough to go to college or unlucky enough to spend time in hospital won't leave either saddled with debt the size of a small mortgage.

When I read about the cost of parenting kids a few years ago, it struck the fear of God into me about my bank balance and my wife's plans for number three.

A knee-jerk reaction, perhaps. Most new dads, whatever their circumstances, attach a sense of self-worth to their ability to provide.

Young new dads have it the hardest. They face big compromises between advancing their careers or education and caring for their family. It can seem unfair suddenly finding yourself a dad in need of extra cash and short on time to earn it. As they grow older, things get easier.

A lack of regular income was a big issue when Sam was little, and I wandered from one low-paying job to the next and even spent a year unemployed. By the time K was born, we'd achieved a measure of financial security.

Thanks to a good salary and living a little under our means, we'd put the days of scrounging for spare change behind the couch and working multiple stressful, low-paying jobs back-to-back behind us. A nice house. Two cars. Holidays under a hot, foreign sun.

But I still struggled with the mental scar tissue of unemployment and the financial crisis of 2008. When the whole endeavour capsizes again, no one will bail out regular families.

The government and the banks might even come looking for more. Ministers of state will get on television in fancy suits and sharp ties and dress up what they're doing using fancy words like "in the national interest" or "we're all in this together".

Only 1 per cent of the population is immune to the cyclical nature of boom-and-bust recessions.

Conscious Spending

"I like nice things, Dad," Sam announced at dinner one night. "And I've a big birthday coming up."

"Don't we all. What is it you want this year?"

"Headphones for running, the new FIFA game and a Philips Hue light and..."

"Stop, stop. I'm sorry I asked."

"How am I going to get them?"

He had me on that one.

Teenagers sometimes get what they want because they've more free time than their parents to develop the right arguments. They work on a mam, dad or grandparent, and Christmas and birthdays are extra leverage.

Sam was a few short years away from going out into the jungle, and he needed to learn some basic financial skills like money management. After all, nothing forms good and bad habits like money (or lack thereof). So, we agreed on a monthly allowance. I wrote up a list of his weekly jobs on our family whiteboard.

Walk the dog.

"Every morning?"

"Every morning."

Clean up the garden on Saturday after the dog.

"That's disgusting."

"That's what we're paying you for."

Take out and bring in the bins.

"Can't you do that one?"

"I could, but then you won't get paid. We'd hate for that to happen."

I set up a standing order for Sam's pocket money and only threatened to cut him off once or twice when he forgot to take out the bins.

He saved up for a few weeks and then complained that he was getting nowhere fast.

"The thing is, I want a lot of things. It's taking too long."

"Write down a list of all the things you want," I said.

"But when will I get them?" he said. "I can't wait till I've enough money. I don't have enough."

"When I was your age, I wanted a lot of things too, but you can't get everything you want," I said. "Let your list sit there for a few days and then decide which one you're going to work towards."

"I don't know, Dad, that sounds like a pretty crappy idea."

"What you want today isn't necessarily what you'll want tomorrow," I said.

"I will. I know it. I need all of these things. They're important to me."

I wanted to teach him not to buy something because it's on sale, stocks are limited, and the "Buy Now" button is large, red and tempting. I needed him to embrace conscious spending.

Perhaps I was expecting too much. It was a hard concept for me to swallow, let alone a fourteen-year-old who knew I had an Amazon Prime subscription.

The ability to stream an album or film instantly, fact-check random dad facts and search for bargains with his smartphone didn't help my case.

Headphones, a football jersey, Bluetooth speakers, a laptop, an iPad, a video game... over a few weeks, Sam's list grew and grew. For kicks, he even added a Tesla and explained the basic model had come down in price.

"It's only €40,000, Dad. You should save up. Get rid of that red banger you keep outside the house."

"My 1995 Toyota Corolla was a steal."

(As I worked from home, we only needed one good family car. I kept this older second car as a reminder that new isn't always better.)

"It's a disgrace. I'm embarrassed when you pick me up from football in it."

"Why not run to training?"

"It's five miles away."

Sam wrote his list and let it steep like a teabag. After a few weeks, he removed several items because they were too expensive or he didn't want them anymore. Finally, he whittled down his list to a few items and then just one.

The Delicate Art of Negotiating With Kids

"I'm looking at these Apple AirPod Pros. They're noise-cancelling. It's the only thing on my list. Can you believe it?"

"I believe they're noise-cancelling. I don't believe the price tag."

"And?"

"I wish you had a job to pay for them."

I explained to my wannabe audiophile son the amount of pocket money to set aside each week. And I wrote down how much he'd need to take from his birthday savings.

He looked at the figures.

"That will take months," he said.

"Some things are worth saving for. Anyway, not many fourteen-year-olds have noise-cancelling earphones."

"I like nice things."

"Somebody has to pay for all these nice things."

"Can you?"

One Saturday afternoon, the five of us went shopping

for Christmas presents in a busy department store in Dublin city centre.

Sam wandered down to the electronics department, next to all the toys, and asked the assistant about AirPods Pro.

"Do you commute?" she asked.

"No, why?"

"Noise-cancelling isn't that useful when you're at home because it's usually quiet. You can hear the music playing with the basic model, no problem."

You don't know life in our house.

While they were talking, K climbed into a giant red toy car and banged the horn for all its worth.

"Beep! Beep! Beep!" he shouted.

The sales assistant looked around as if to say: "Is he yours?"

Meanwhile, Audrey tried and failed to extract him from the front seat.

"Dad, if I pay half for the cheaper ones, will you pay the other half?" Sam asked.

"When I was a little older than you, I worked for hours in a supermarket. They paid me just €1.98 an hour..." I said. "Do you know how long it takes to earn half a million euros on €1.98 an hour?"

"I'm not old enough to get a part-time job."

Damn our employment laws!

"I can do a few more jobs around the house," he said. "I'll walk the dog, empty the dishwasher..."

We came to a reluctant agreement.

Little-known Investment Strategies for Broke Dads

Sam enjoyed overspending his free time on Amazon, finding inspiring ways to dent our bank balance. Fearing bankruptcy, I shared access to several online courses I'd bought over the past few years. One of them explained how to start an online business.

"Invest in yourself, and you'll never go broke," I said.

And I won't have to bail you out of financial jam later on.

But he was too busy listening to music on his new AirPods. I forgot about the courses for a while. Then one evening, he marched into the kitchen and announced: "I watched a few of those videos. I want to buy one about dropshipping. It's on Udemy."

"Isn't everything for sale on Udemy?"

"It's €20, Dad."

I knew little about dropshipping, but I paid for the course anyway, so he'd have something constructive to do rather than figuring out what's on sale on Amazon and how quickly he could hit the order button.

A few nights later, I caught him sitting at the kitchen table, watching videos from the course and taking actual notes.

Don't make any sudden movements. We're witnessing something very rare: a teenager engaged in self-directed learning!

That evening Sam cornered me in the kitchen and said, "I need to buy a domain name for my Shopify store. Can you pay for it?"

"Does this mean I'm a seed investor?"

"A what?"

I agreed to cover the cost of setting up his store on

Shopify. He wanted to earn money, so he could spend it. I wanted him to spend a little money so he could learn how to earn it.

We met somewhere in the messy middle.

"Look, Dad," he said. "If my store works out and I make sales, I'm moving to Los Angeles."

His Just Rewards

Sam called his business Manor Fitness, after the estate where we live (The Manor). He spent hours at night and over the weekend designing a logo and page templates. He also set up sales pages for resistance bands and home-gym fitness equipment dropshipped from China.

"Can I have your credit card?" he asked one afternoon when I got in from a long run.

"For what? More headphones?"

"I want to run Facebook ads."

"Facebook ads?"

"How else am I going to make sales?"

Over dinner, he also started asking me questions like, "What can I do about the twenty-to-forty-day wait for deliveries from China?"

Sam didn't sell any products, but I was happy to bankroll the cost of his self-directed learning. He closed down Manor Fitness after a few months and moved on to take online courses in web design and coding.

The *Bhagavad Gita* says we're entitled to our labour but not the fruits of our labour.

That's a good rule for dads. You're entitled to act as their teacher, banker and chauffeur but don't always expect something in return.

Instead of explaining my crazy theories to Sam, I

congratulated him on finishing things: a garden free of dog crap, weights in a gym tidied way, and an online course put to good use.

"That's how you'll get what you want," I said.

"I get it, Dad, I really do," he said. "So I'm thinking about buying shares in Tesla..."

Takeaways

Alongside the sex talk, money is an important conversation to have with your kids.

Unless your family is loaded, they'll spend a large portion of their lives working at jobs they loathe, love and feel ambivalent about to provide for themselves and even a family of their own. A stack of cash won't buy them ever-lasting happiness, but it will buy a degree of freedom, for a college course, starting a business or buying a place to live.

What chores can you give to your kids to earn a little? Can you teach them to save up for something they want instead of blowing their cash as soon as they get it? Will you give them pocket money for a job well done and, if so, how much?

Money is a useful tool for teaching concepts like delayed gratification, the value of hard work and how to give back. It also helps if kids understand they don't have to spend every cent as soon as they get it.

Money Tips... Cha-Ching!

- Start paying your son or daughter a weekly allowance. It's a great motivational tool and a useful means of teaching them about money.

- If they've outgrown a savings box, set up a savings account. When they get older, family and even friends will give them cash for presents. Cultivating a savings habit is good practice.
- Don't be afraid to dock their pocket money if they skip their chores for a few days. It's easier and more effective than a shouting match or argument.

TWENTY-FIVE

BEST FRIENDS

Vodka and coke, please.
Down in one, and up I heave,
Retching on my knees.

Teenagers count on their friends, but they also need authority figures. Like it or not, that's a dad's job.

"You could try sneaking some vodka from your parent's house?" said Daire.

A best friend from school, Daire had dark hair, brown eyes, and everything about him was deliberate and thought-through.

"I dunno if that's a good idea," I said. "My mam will find out."

"That's what I'm doing," he said. "Top the vodka bottle up with a little water. They'll never find out."

He paused.

"I will if you will."

"I dunno Daire..."

"Do you want to get pissed?"

"I want to get pissed!"

Daire flashed a broad smile. With dark hair gel and a pressed, immaculate Ralph Lauren shirt, he'd more experience drinking and with girls than me.

We were sixteen, and it was the night before a big disco at the local No Name club.[1] Several of my friends secured alcohol in advance. They used fake IDs or asked their parents to buy them drinks. I'd no idea where to get a fake ID, much less a parent who would buy me an alcoholic drink.

On the night of the disco, my parents went out with friends for dinner. After they left, I turned the key on the large wooden cabinet where they kept their drinks.

The bottles of spirits – Jameson, Smirnoff, Baileys – glittered like bronze, silver and gold medals. Small cans of Heineken lined the top shelf, but they wouldn't do. I'd only tasted beer a few times and found it bitter and gassy. And besides, cans were awkward to carry, let alone sneak into a teenage disco.

I took out the whiskey bottle, poured a drop into the cap and took a sip. I retched almost immediately. Next, I took out the bottle of Baileys. The seal was unbroken, so that was out.

Then, I took an open litre bottle of Smirnoff vodka from the cabinet, held it into the air and inspected the clear white liquid.

This has to be easier than drinking beer or whiskey.

Even if I somehow smuggled a litre bottle of vodka into

the disco, my parents would notice its absence the following day.

I needed a way of transporting the alcohol discreetly with me into the disco. But I couldn't find any smaller plastic bottles in the kitchen.

What would Daire do?

I searched around the house for empty bottles and couldn't find any (this was back in 1997 before plastic bottles of water were popular).

Upstairs in the bathroom, I squeezed out the last of the shampoo from a plastic container and rinsed it out a few times. I filled the bottle up with water and took a slug to see if I could taste shampoo. I sloshed water around my mouth and swallowed. Pleased, I filled it with vodka and 7Up. Then, I carefully topped up the vodka bottle with water and put it back in the drinks cabinet. In the shower, I drank from the shampoo bottle, delighted with the warm feeling filling my chest.

They'll never know.

Daire's dad picked me up from the house to drive us to the disco. Three of my friends were already inside the car.

"I've sprung a leak!" whispered Daire.

He tapped the conspicuous bulge of a bottle in his jean pocket. We started laughing. His dad frowned at us from the rear-review mirror and I bit my lip.

After he'd dropped us off, we walked from the disco entrance towards a quiet field at the other end of the college campus.

"We're finally on the piss,"[2] said Daire.

"Yesssss, you better believe it. Look what I have, lads." I pulled out the shampoo bottle for the others to see. "Want some?"

"Is that a shampoo bottle?" Daire laughed.

"What are you even drinking, Collins?" said another friend. "Fucking L'Oréal?"

"It was all I could find."

A wall of white light enveloped us.

"Evening, lads."

We turned to face a large bald man waving a torch at us. His breath formed clouds above the security badge on his high-vis jacket and rose into the autumn air.

"Out for a walk?"

"We're just..." said Daire.

Before I could stuff the shampoo bottle into my jeans, he stepped forwards, snatched it from me, opened the bottle and sniffed.

"An unusual choice, young man," he said. "Follow back with me to the club. I'll call your parents. Let them know what you lads are really up to out here."

We walked ahead of him in silence towards the disco.

Busted.

I was going to get into more trouble than I'd ever encountered. At the disco, the security guard took bottles of drink from the rest of the lads and dumped them into a wheelie bin.

"Go on inside. I'll be watching," he said.

He pushed open the double doors, and we walked in – triumph and disaster in equal measure.

I woke up the following morning and ate breakfast with my parents. After they left for an afternoon shopping trip, I tried studying for a maths exam, but the image of a vodka bottle kept appearing before me.

I'd almost completed a rite of passage. I'd come so tantalising close to getting drunk.

That half-full vodka bottle was still in the drinks cabinet.

Why not try a little more...?

I didn't bother with a shampoo bottle or even 7-Up this time. I filled a large glass and gulped it down.

An hour later, playing music, I shook the bottle, surprised that it was almost empty.

I filled the whole bottle up with water.

The doorbell rang. Daire wanted to catch up about last night.

"That was a close one," he said. "I don't know how we got away with it."

"I'm still getting away with it, Daire." I threw my hands up in the air. "Look at me. I'm drunk!"

Inside, he saw puddles of water on the kitchen floor and a bottle of vodka by the sink.

"Jesus Bryan, you're locked," [3] he said. "You better sober up before your parents get home."

"You better believe it!"

"Some fresh air might help."

I remember little about the walk apart from holding onto someone's garden wall and retching vodka onto my trainers.

Daire deposited me back at home before it got dark. I was lying on the couch, my head spinning when my parents returned.

My mother walked in and turned on the lights.

"What's wrong with you?" she said.

"There'ssh nofing, there'ssh nofingwrong with me, whash wrang with you?"

"Pat," my mam said. "Pat, I think he's drunk."

They put me to bed early and cleaned up some vomit on the kitchen floor.

If getting drunk was an Irish rite of passage, I'd staggered through the front door, tripped over myself and fallen on my ass.

I'm Your Dad, Not Your Friend

A friend without kids asked me once, "If Bryan in his early twenties could meet Bryan now, how do you think they'd get on?"

"He'd be horrified."

It's not my job to become friends with the child-free me from fifteen-plus years ago. I also suspect anyone who confuses friendship with parenting of conflicting priorities.

A friend says, "I will if you will." A dad tells the kids, "I don't, so you won't."

Friends don't enjoy arguing with each other. A spirited debate is OK.

New dads need more paid parental leave.

Legalise the weed. Here's why.

Has anyone ever tried communism?

I like the cut of your jib.[4] *How may I join your newsletter?*

But an argument implies a fundamental difference of opinion or an uneven balance of power. That's hard for relationships to recover from.

It's different with families. Like Peter Parker, parents are meant to have more power than the kids. Like Spiderman, wield it lightly.

For a few weeks one summer, Sam and I enjoyed the same argument at dinner every evening.

"I want to cycle with my friends out to Kilcock tomorrow afternoon," he said.

Kilcock is about five miles out from Maynooth, and his

proposed trip involved cycling along the canal bank or a busy road.

A friend would have said, "What a great idea. Let's do it. Bring snacks. I'll meet you on the way!"

On the one hand, I wanted Sam to spend less time living online with virtual FIFA buddies and more time out with real-world friends. On the other hand, I imagined tyre blowouts. I thought of all the swimming classes he skipped. I remembered a local tragedy I covered years ago as a journalist and watching emergency services fish a body out of the canal.

I worried about what his friends were up to, alone on the canal. At least Sam was at home playing video games. I knew his whereabouts.

"It's too far for you, and I know your friends are swimming in the canal," I said. "I spotted them near the water while out for a run."

"Those weren't my friends."

"They had your fringe."

"Dad! Come on... everyone is going." He waved his phone in the air as proof. "Look, you can even read my WhatsApp messages."

"If everyone jumped into the... wait, wait, that's not the right example. Look, I said no."

And around we went.

Eventually, we came to a compromise.

Sam could meet his friends for a few hours provided he kept his phone on, checked in on WhatsApp, returned at a set time and, "Don't go near the water!"

Takeaways

A best friend doesn't decide what's acceptable. Instead, they say, "I will if you will."

Our kids deserve best friends. But they need authority figures, for a few years at least. They respond well through understanding where the boundaries lie if only to test them.

Parents worry about what happens when their teenagers first meet the temptations of the adult world: alcohol, drugs, sex and, now, the Internet. You can lock up the drinks cabinet and talk to them about sex, but it's all but impossible to protect them from every potential vice and danger.

Take the Internet. Even if you can control access at home, they'll eventually find a way online in their friends' houses or at school. Better to give them the skills they need to navigate real and virtual worlds, like understanding privacy, standing up for themselves and showing respect to more vulnerable people.

Rules and clear expectations help too.

Older teenagers tire of submitting to family rules. They believe, "I've got this figured out. I know what to do. I'm old enough. Why should I listen to you anymore?"

Some mature teenagers are right. They're usually the ones who drop out of a paid college scholarship to set up the next billion-dollar company, and all before they turn twenty-one.

The rest of us drive smack-bang into other authority figures that are less understanding than any parent.

Dads Vs. Friends Tips

- It's easy to keep track of your child's friends when they're small and call to the house. It's harder when they start navigating a hectic social life with a smartphone. Insist on their friends' first and last names, phone numbers of parents and times they'll return home at.
- Technically, you're entitled to take your teenage son or daughter's phone and investigate its contents. Consider it a nuclear option. It's a surefire way to destroy trust between a dad and his growing son or daughter.

TWENTY-SIX

THE PLAN

Taller than your mother,
Clean your bum, shave your moustache.
Christ, how fast was that?

A dad's interests, hobbies and pursuits rub off on his children in surprising and unexpected ways.

"What are those?" Sam asked me one evening.

I was clobbering around the kitchen in a pair of noisy, heavy weightlifting shoes.

"They stop me from falling over when I'm in the gym," I said.

"Falling over from what?"

"When I'm squatting with the barbell."

Sam's eyes widened.

A few months before, our neighbour built a home gym

and gave me a key. It contained a squat rack, barbell, kettle-bells, weights and enough space for one person to work out.

On Tuesday and Friday evenings, while Audrey watched *X-Factor*, I trained in the gym for an hour after work.

"Show me!"

"Not tonight."

"When?"

"Perhaps when you're older."

"That'll take too long."

The following Tuesday, while in the middle of dead-lifts, I caught Sam peering in the small window.

He tapped on the glass.

"Can I come in?"

"No, I'm trying to work out here!"

He opened the door and stepped inside.

"I want to use the barbell, Dad."

"You're not old enough."

"Show me."

"Go on back inside."

Sam reappeared outside the home gym the following session taking notes, kind of like a stray dog wandering into a garden expecting scraps of food.

"Please, Dad, I'm ready."

"No, I've been working all day, and I need a break. Why don't you go for a run?"

"I don't want to run. I want to use the gym."

"You could get hurt."

"I'll go in when you're working tomorrow."

"You will not."

"You can't stop me!"

"You're probably right."

I closed the door, having learnt long ago to avoid a power struggle with him.

"Why won't you show him?" Audrey asked me later that evening.

"He's fourteen. I don't know if he's old enough to strength train. He could fall over and hurt himself. Next thing, he'll be looking for protein powder, and we'll have to pay for that too."

"Don't be ridiculous. He's not going to want protein powder," she said.

But that wasn't the real reason. Who was I to teach something I'd only learnt a few months ago at the local CrossFit gym? Besides, running and now strength training were my ways of unwinding after work and outside of the family unit.

Still, Sam would win gold in an event for persistence. He's studied, refined and practised this skill against both parents for fourteen years.

He'd also spent the past year watching Netflix documentaries about ripped champion CrossFitters like Rich Froning and Mat Fraser.

On the one hand, I liked that he'd found a new set of sporting heroes to emulate. On the other, I worried about all the body-conscious messages Instagram was sending his generation. When my friends and I were his age, we spent more time wondering about how to score cheap booze than sculpting a six-pack.

After I finished a workout one evening, he cornered me in the kitchen with questions about YouTube weightlifting videos.

"I can do it, Dad, I'm old enough. I'll practise every night. These guys aren't much older than I am."

I checked his YouTube playlist.

The Official Deadlift Checklist.

How to Power Clean (Olympic Weightlifting 101).

Squats for Beginners: How to Do a Squat Correctly.

I even picked up a few tips from his Internet research.

"Instagram and YouTube aren't reality," I said. "You can't live life with a filter on."

"Your CrossFit gym would let me in," he said.

"They would not. You need to be sixteen to join. It's for insurance."

"Ah, Dad, no one cares about that," he said.

"I'm sure their insurers do."

"I'm sending them an email to see if I can join."

"You have to be sixteen…"

"I'll tell them I'm sixteen!"

Concession Time

"I got you something," I said to Sam one evening. "You're going to love it."

"What?"

"It's a book."

"A book? You know I don't like reading, Dad."

"It's called *Starting Strength*. [1] Why don't you read a few chapters."

"Reading? Ugh."

"Your sister reads books every night."

"Yeah, picture books."

"That still counts. It's about weightlifting."

"I don't have time for books," said Sam. "I want to lift weights and deadlift and power clean."

"If you want to lift weights," I said, tapping on the Kindle, "start here. Think of it as your mental warm-up. This book will prepare you for the basics."

"Is this where you learnt?"

Actually, son, the coach at the gym kept telling me to take the weight down and stand up straight. I fell on my ass for months.

Critics say weight training impedes a teenager's growth, but fourteen-year-olds can safely train once they reduce the weight.

My son joined the local gym, but his instructor prepared a complex plan that he couldn't follow and didn't enjoy. He also wasn't quite old enough to join the local CrossFit gym, where I learnt the basics of strength training.

Sam stood a better chance of learning good form in-person rather than by scrubbing through YouTube videos of buff CrossFitters, even if I'm hopelessly uncoordinated.

I also a discovered an important lesson about strength training: it teaches a kind of grit. While squatting under a heavy bar, you either stand up or land on your ass.

Surviving heavy sets builds confidence, something I needed when I was his age and even after he arrived. Perhaps, it's a dad's job to teach their children the skills they need to build themselves up.

Or perhaps he's more persistent than I am.

Hold My Sweeping Brush

Sam lifted the steel barbell off the rack, wobbled beneath the twenty-kilo weight and almost crashed against the window.

"Put down that barbell," I said. "You're not ready for it."

"But, I've read the book."

"We still need to drill the exercises."

So I deconstructed what I knew about learning to lift weights from my rather unreliable memory. "We're going to practice with this," I said, pulling out an old broom from the corner of the gym.

"What the hell is that? I want to use a barbell!"

"That's how I learnt. We practised our form every session before touching a loaded barbell."

"It's a broom!"

"Follow the plan."

He drilled the movements, worked with the broom for a few days. I recorded his movements with a phone and pointed out when he should straighten his back or drive with his hips.

Then, we moved on to twelve-kilogram kettlebells before he finally picked up the barbell. He practised with and without me and logged his lifts in the official *Starting Strength* app.

He trained three or four evenings a week alongside football practice with his team. I admired his determination. When my generation were teenagers, we spent our free time figuring out how to buy alcohol and binge drink in fields without our parents finding out.

One evening, after the gym, he walked into the kitchen and plodded around in Under Armour gear.

"Is there any pasta left?" He peered in the fridge.

"Show me your stats," I said.

He opened the app and thumbed through a chart on his phone depicting his deadlift and squat benchmarks.

"It looks like you're training three times a week."

"That's what the plan says."

"Well done."

"Thanks."

"I wish you'd clean your jacks[2] with the same sense of purpose."

He took to the plan with the intensity of an investigative

journalist, asking me questions about his form, technique lift and when to add weights to the bar.

"How much do you lift?" he asked me.

"More than you."

And:

"My hands are hurting from the barbell. What should I do about it?"

Don't get me started on the calluses.

Babies and small kids are like sponges, soaking up most of their parents' time and attention directly. They're hungry, in need of attention or tired. Your job is to feed them, play with them or settle them to sleep.

Teenage boys are more subtle.

If you ask them to go for a walk down the street, they might say "no", in case one of their friends spots them out with the old man. But they're still paying attention.

They notice their dad's mannerisms and habits, like the odd way you stand while ordering food in a cafe, how you swear in traffic and what you do with free time after work. At least I wasn't in a garden shed drinking bottles of vodka and growing marijuana.

Follow the Plan

One warm Saturday evening, the neighbours came over to our house for a BBQ, beers and wine. I cooked steaks, and Audrey prepared potato salad. We sat out in the back garden with the baby, Maria and the neighbour's baby, eating and enjoying the last of the summer heat.

We ate, listening to the crash and bang of weights hitting the padded gym floor, as Sam worked out in the gym next door.

"I'm thinking of charging your son a membership fee," said my neighbour. "He's in there so much."

"Oh, he's consistent alright. He doesn't like letting things go."

"It's something for him to do at night apart from playing *FIFA*," said my wife. "He was always on that Playstation."

"There's nothing wrong with video games," I said. "But yeah, it might be good for him."

Later that night, after we'd tidied up, Sam wandered into the kitchen and picked at the last of the BBQ. Then, he played a video clip of his workout for me.

"How's my form?"

"It's getting better, but follow the training plan. Keep practising."

"What do I need to practise? When will I know how to do it?"

"Think of it like hurling drills or a game to play. You're never really done."

"So what should I do?"

"Keep going."

"Look, I have this other video... check out my power cleans."

I scraped some chicken wings into the bin.

"Don't waste that food!" he said.

While he ate, I watched several videos of Sam practising power cleans and deadlifts.

"Try to drive with your hips more."

"What about this one?"

He pressed his phone into my hands.

"Can we stop talking about power cleans? It's nearly midnight, I'm tired, and I'm going to bed."

"Alright, alright, but before you go..."

"What?"

"I need some protein powder."

Takeaways

It's easy to set boundaries with small children, assuming you can handle the temper tantrums and agree on an approach with their mother or your partner .

A dad tells his young child, "No!", sets rules and limits. And they might listen!

Good luck enforcing that with a teenager. Even if you could monitor them 24/7, would you want to? Too many constraints set them up for failure later in life. After all, they need to learn how to bear the weight of a metaphorical barbell without your help. Expect them to look towards you, their older friends, sporting heroes, the guy next door and people they follow online.

As dads, we worry they're looking in the wrong direction. Sam's generation spends an inordinate amount of time online shaping their identities, for better or worse. Thanks to Instagram, his generation are more body-conscious than we ever were.

I'm under no illusions; vanity comes with a price.

But sports, whether it's weightlifting, football, tennis or running, builds a better sense of self than drinking cans of Dutch Gold in a field after school.

It also helps them forge their sense of self.

The biggest challenge for dads of older children is figuring out how much autonomy to give them and when.

They'll find a way to explore what they're curious about. Who will show them: you or someone else?

Tips for Would-be Teachers

- Let your son or daughter take risks within reason. If they don't want your advice, remember teenage boys often look towards other male role models as mentors. Subtly point them in the right direction through coaching, books and even online courses.
- Reforge a bond with your son as they transition from one stage to the next. Dad credits for time spent together in the play centre when they were small expire. You'll both find it easier over a shared activity or a short trip.

TWENTY-SEVEN

PROMISES, PROMISES

I broke a promise to you once.
I'll keep the next one, I swear.

———————

Raising kids puts a few years on every dad. Preparing for tomorrow only gets guys so far.

"Who do you think will die first?" said Jon.

I was out in a Dublin City Centre bar with some old school friends one Saturday night. We got around to talking about death, as you do at two in the morning, after a few beers.

Anto, coming up on forty with a thick mane of dark hair, took in the question, looked around the table and settled his gaze on me.

"Bryan," he said.

"What? Why? Don't you know I'm working out, lifting

weights, running, meditating. I've got my shit under control..."

"It's the stress of all those kids you have," he said. "It's not good for you."

I sipped my beer. "I'm feeling pretty good, Anto."

"Look at me, I've no kids, thank God," he said. "I get up late on Sunday when I want, play golf and go for a massage and maybe have a bottle of wine with the missus or go to bed early. How's your Sunday looking?"

"I get up when the kids get up. Football matches, family dinners, dance practice. They keep us busy."

We laughed.

"I don't know how you do it," he said.

"The day goes fast," I said. "Sometimes, too fast. Now that you mention it, I better get off home. I've to collect Sam from football training in the morning."

We're Living In Communist Russia

Child-free friends with no desire to have kids, like Anto, look at families with 2.5 kids, a dog and a picket fence and wonder how we do it. I look at larger families with five, six or even seven kids, and I wonder how *they* do it.

I've a working theory: raising each kid puts five years on their fathers.

Or perhaps on me.

I've a library of family photos from the last decade on my phone. Thumbing through them is like watching the last fifteen years of my life flashing past my eyes, a type of near-death experience.

There's me in Ibiza on my stag. There's me with Sam at a West Ham football match. There's me feeding Maria her first bottle.

When I reach the photographs of bewildered me holding a newborn baby in a maternity ward, I'm shocked by my thick black hair and my immaculate crown, free of wrinkles and frown lines. Perhaps Anto was right. Perhaps creating a child takes something essential out of us? Or perhaps it's the passage of time?

I know this much. New parents expect too much of themselves. It's one part terrifying and another part breathtaking to hold a pink, wriggling, helpless baby that's dependent on *you*. (Admittedly, for the first year or two, the baby is more dependent on his or her mother. Dads are kind of like the vice-president in a non-profit venture.)

Perhaps that explains why new dads make impossible promises we've every intention of keeping.

A few days after Maria was born, I set her down on a pink blanket on the couch. She wrapped her small fingers around my thumb, pulled her chubby legs towards her chest and sucked her lip.

"I won't let anything bad happen to you," I whispered.

Most dads have similar experiences. They want to keep their son or daughter safe from all the harm in the world. It should be easy, right?

The job expectations are clear for the first few years. Don't let them fall into the fire, eat raw chicken or stick forks in the plug sockets. Stop them from eating food off the floor (less than five seconds is OK), taking dishwasher tablets from the kitchen press and falling down the stairs.

But then the job expectations change. Playing dad to a toddler in a nuclear family is kind of like living in communist Russia.

If in with the party faithful, only you can plámás the child and comfort him or her.[1] Walk into the room, and they'll smile and run into your arms, their entire world before them.

The following day, you're still the same guy, but now when you walk into the room, they run away waving their hands in the air, shouting "No Daddy!" and calling out "Mam!"

Only she will suffice.

If this were a Russian purge, you're on the way to Siberia.

My friend Anto believes young or new parents lead busier, more stressful lives than their child-free counterparts. I suspect he's right, but most parents wouldn't swap their new lives for their old ones. Still, dad promises should come with an expiry date or at least a health warning.

With toddlerhood under control, the parenting game changes up again. A dad has to teach their kids how to cross the road alone, when to trust (or ignore) a stranger, and what to do if someone contacts them online. A promise to keep them safe also means allowing them to learn from their mistakes, develop their values and a sense of autonomy.

The well-intentioned dad who tries to keep an ancient promise to protect their son or daughter is doing them an active disservice; how will they ever learn to survive in the real world with somebody to catch them every time they fall?

A dad can point their son or daughter's moral compass in the right direction, but the adult child must recalibrate based on their values with their friends, bosses, partners, and perhaps a family of their own.

Stuff It, Dad

Teenagers, rapidly approaching the cusp of adulthood, search for freedom... mostly from their parents. They don't care much for a parent's promises unless they're broken. They'll also happily point out when Mum or Dad is at fault.

One September, our family spent a few days in Center Parcs, a popular outdoor holiday centre, in Co. Longford.

On the last day, I was minding my business, packing up the car to drive home, like one of those guys in a crowded Japanese metro station who gets paid to stuff people into the carriage at rush hour. [2]

A raised teenage voice rang out from the lodge next door to ours.

"...you promised me you wouldn't do this."

"Don't talk to me like that," came a weary reply. "You have a real attitude about it!"

"Stuff it, Dad!"

A lanky sixteen-year-boy with curly black hair barged out of the wooden lodge and stormed down the road.

His dad stepped out on the front porch and called out after his son for a bit before going back inside to his other kids. Or perhaps he sat down on the couch and enjoyed the peace and quiet.

I found the dynamics of an older family fighting in public about who said what, to whom and when amusing.

Rather them than us.

Two minutes later, my oldest son stormed out of our lodge and onto the road.

"Maaaam, where did you put my headphones?!"

"They're in the empty bag."

"What bloody empty bag?" he shouted in the middle of the road. "Dad's packing up the car. This is a joke."

Sam tried to pull out some bags I'd stuffed into the boot.

"Don't touch the bags!" I said. "I spent half an hour getting them in just right."

"Maaaam!"

The two of them gathered behind the car and consulted on my packing style.

"You packed up the car all wrong," said Audrey.

"I can manage. I don't need a degree to put suitcases in a car," I said.

My argument fell apart when I tried to close the boot, and two suitcases fell out onto the ground.

"I can't get my headphones," said Sam.

"Maybe if you'd packed up your stuff the night before like we agreed..." I said.

And like that, we put on a show for an older couple on the other side of our lodge, sipping coffee on their front porch and admiring other people's problems on a fine autumn morning.

Promises Undone

One Wednesday evening, an old friend from work rang. She was upset.

"It's Veronica," said Mary. "She's, she's died."

"What do you mean she died?" I said. "Are you sure? There must be some mistake?"

Mary began to cry.

"She died. Her daughter found her lying on the bathroom floor. She never woke up. It's terrible..."

Veronica and I worked together, her as a nurse and me as a care worker, in the same community house for three years. I didn't know her well outside the job, but shift work brings people together in unexpected ways.

Our small team clocked in at eight a.m. and out at nine p.m. for two or three days straight. Spend that much time with someone, and you'll get them to know them pretty quick.

Veronica brought a large black handbag into work, stuffed with magazines about the soaps, to read on her break. During the day, we helped the residents at day services or dropped them at school, work or their doctors' appointments.

Evenings were quieter.

After dinner, Veronica sat watching soaps like *Coronation Street* and *EastEnders* with the residents while we filled out paperwork and complained about the management's latest policies and procedures.

If the office phone rang after hours, Veronica joked, "This better be a medical emergency!"

Veronica was several years older than me, and she loved to ask me about Maria's sleeping habits.

"And is Maria sleeping at night? Oh, isn't it great when they sleep at night! My two never slept. You're so lucky."

I told her I'd taken up running.

"I ran the women's mini-marathon last year. My arches fell. Never again."

Once, she even confessed: "I'm going to go into that doctor tomorrow, and I'll tell him I'm not getting postnatal depression with the next baby."

Her funeral took place on the hottest day of the year. The small country church couldn't hold all of her friends and family, let alone people from work. So, I sat with the old team on rocks outside the church, sweating into my white shirt and wiping my brow with a tie. The priest delivered a bland eulogy over speakers that offered no trace of her personality.

We went to the pub afterwards and swapped stories about Veronica. A warm, strong and competent nurse, we'd lots to trade.

"Do you know she drove home on her lunch break to put on a wash and a dinner for the kids?" said Mary.

"I'll never forget her Friday lunchtime sagas with the women in the AIB bank and her refusal to use Internet banking!" said another friend.

"What will happen to the kids now?" I said.

"Her husband will raise them, I suppose," said Mary.

We couldn't find any sense or logic in a five-year-old and two-year-old growing up without their mother.

A parent promises to keep their son or daughter safe, to raise them well and see them out into the world.

A career, a mortgage, a permanent job, kids, plans for the future and the little people who need you, promises made, and some kept... but none of it is any protection.

The day after the funeral, I drove home tired, drained, promising to myself to update my will.

Years ago, after Sam was born, I lost sleep worrying about one of us dying accidentally and him growing up without a parent. Veronica's death was a difficult reminder. But I was also here.

I was alive.

I pulled up outside our front door and met my next-door neighbour taking pink balloons and nappies out of his car.

"Bryan," he said, lifting the balloons in the air and smiling. "We've had a baby girl!"

Takeaways

You'll promise many things to your kids over the years and with the best intentions of keeping every one. But the reality is it's impossible to avoid breaking a promise and letting those close to you down. Some of them should come with an expiry date.

When your family outgrows a rule, habit or old promise, cast it aside. We all live in a state of constant change, and that includes family life.

You can't protect your kids from every misfortune, but you can mark big events with them. Kids need the skills and resources to survive without their parent's help or even their presence.

Tips to Swear By

- Be wary of speaking in negative absolutes with kids, for example, "You never...", "You can't...", and "You won't..." They don't respond well to them (nor do adults!).
- Morbid alert! Dads need a will, even if you don't have much to leave behind. With your partner, figure out what will happen if one or both of you unexpectedly pass away.

TWENTY-EIGHT
BREATHE

Sit, focus, breathe.
Impossible with this monkey mind,
Running through my house.

Parenting is immensely rewarding, but the inevitable stresses of family life take their toll. Best seek a means of recharging.

"I wish you'd hurry up," said the mother beside us.

"You kids are taking too long. We haven't got all day. Pick one, so I can pay the lady and we can go."

Maria and I were standing in a giant Lego playhouse at the back of a bookstore in Co. Wexford, browsing books, Lego adventure sets while Audrey shopped for lunch with the baby.

The three kids beside the stressed-out mother looked under nine. Her youngest son picked up a Lego *Star Wars* box off the shelf, examined the Death Star with the intensity of a Luke Skywalker, and put it back on the shelf. Next, the boy picked up an *Indiana Jones* Temple Escape Lego kit.

He studied the back of the box, put it down and picked up another. I admired his tenacity. He cared nothing for his mother standing behind him with one hand on her hip tapping her watch.

Meanwhile, I pretended to study the back cover of a book, *The Bodhisattva's Way of Life*. It explained how practising patience is key to finding enlightenment.

"The lady in the shop isn't going to let you build them here," she said. "Pick one, so we can go."

"But Mam, I don't know which one I want. There are so many."

Tap. Tap. Tap.

"Just pick one, please. I'm losing the will to live here."

"But..."

Tap. Tap. Tap.

"Maaaaaaam!"

"That's it, love," she said. "I've officially lost the will to live. I'm walking away right now and leaving your kids here. Don't try to stop me. I've had it. I'm going. I'm going."

"Mam, you wouldn't."

Tap. Tap. Tap.

"Last chance."

"Noooo!"

She walked towards the door, calling out... "Ten, nine, eight, seven...."

The smallest boy looked towards his disappearing mother and back at the floor-to-ceiling green, red, and yellow shelves stacked with Lego sets. She continued walking down the steps of the playhouse and towards the exit.

I wanted to call out, "You're on the right track, lady. Even the Buddha walked away." I'd leave out the bit about how he left his wife and kids to embark on a great spiritual journey and sit under a tree. Then my phone rang.

"What's taking you so long, Bryan? The baby is hungry."

"Taking so long? I thought we were meeting at... oh wait, is it that time already?"

I could almost hear the tapping sound over the phone.

The Bodhisattva's Way of Life says, "practising patience is key to finding enlightenment". [1]

Enlightenment. In the car on the way home, I could have done with some of that.

In the middle of a traffic jam, the baby began roaring, and the other two started fighting about not having enough space to stretch out their legs and arms towards every corner.

"Mam, he's taking up all the room!"

"Keep your feet over your own side."

I thought about losing the will to live and opening the car door, but I'd nowhere to go.

... And Breathe

Somewhere between an unexpected event and three kids, a picket fence and a dog, I learned how to sit on a cushion and do... nothing. If you'd asked me in my early twenties to close my eyes and focus on my breath for five or ten minutes, let alone twenty, I'd have laughed and asked for another beer.

Over the years, I've read a few books about Zen, but I'd

never consciously tried to meditate. Then my hamstrings and glutes began locking up after long runs.

"Why don't you try yoga?" suggested a more agile club member. "It loosened me right up."

The first time I took a yoga class, I was pleasantly surprised when the teacher asked us to lie on the ground for a few minutes at the end of practice. It was like a nice rest after a moderate workout.

"Focus on the breath. In and out. In and out. If it helps, count slowly backwards from ten and repeat. Savasana."

Savasana...

I rolled the word around in my head. It had an almost mystical quality to it.

A moment of stillness once a week wasn't enough, though. I still caught myself on the verge of losing it more often than not.

One day, I watched a YouTube video of a meditation teacher with a shaved head sit cross-legged on a cushion and explain the monkey mind. "It's kind of like an energetic two-year-old, who's always on to the next thing. And the next. The problem is it's impossible to find any peace when you're always onto the next thing."

After watching a few more videos, I spent ten minutes jamming my legs into an awkward position and nearly tore a muscle. Instead, I turned to apps like Headspace and tried meditating for a few minutes each morning.

I told myself learning to meditate would help me get more stuff done at a tough job.

I secretly wanted to find a way of managing my moods better. It was either learn to sit or throw one of the kids out the window.

I stuck with it on and off for a year or two. I must have bored friends or family with my practice because one

Christmas, my wife bought me a voucher for a mindfulness day in a meditation centre in Dublin.

We took part in practices like mindful eating and walking. I didn't enjoy the former, at least in company.

Chomp. Chomp. Chomp.

"Can you pass the... oh wait, sorry."

Chomp. Chomp. Chomp.

A mindful walk in the garden after lunch was easier. We trotted around in circles, admiring the plants.

Trot. Trot. Trot.

"Ah, this is nice."

Trot. Trot. Trot.

After meditating for the day, I came home, changed three broken light bulbs and hung a shelf, DIY jobs I'd put off for weeks.

I spent a weekend on a yoga and meditation retreat in Co. Leitrim a few years later. I was also on point for a big work project that spilt out into my weekend. I left some of the classes early to respond to the barrage of emails and Slack messages, hardly the point of a retreat. Still, the group meditation sessions in the mornings and evenings were like coming home.

"Meditation has no goal," the teacher told us. "It's a practice, that's all."

Kind of like parenting.

The following year, I completed a course in transcendental meditation (TM). This practice involves sitting down and meditating for twenty minutes in the morning and evening, using a mantra (a meaningless sound cultivating inner white noise). The first rule of transcendental meditation is: *Don't talk about transcendental meditation.*

The organisation behind TM advises aspiring students to learn the basics with a teacher. It costs several hundred euros or dollars. A teacher provides a personal mantra and some other instructions.

When I heard about all that, I worried I was joining a cult. It didn't help that I found out TM has its own island in Ireland. But learning TM was easy and came with no strings.

On the first day, I turned up, and the teacher gave me a mantra. We met a further three times and meditated in company with half a dozen other students. And that was it.

No talk of motherships, invites to the island or jumping on a couch with Oprah.

Transcendental meditation helped me go deeper than other practices. I set aside twenty minutes early in the morning before starting work and in the later afternoon or evening. I even booked time in my calendar for mid-afternoon meditation sessions.

The Silence, It's Deafening

If art demands patience, so does raising a kid from zero to eighteen. It's OK to get frustrated with your little Mona Lisas. In fact, it'd be odd if parents didn't.

Frustration implies giving a damn, whereas nonchalance means you're ready to give them up.

Kids are unsure what they want unless their brother or sister has it. Then, they most certainly want it, and more because anything else is painfully unfair.

They don't deal in logic, although they enjoy playing both parents off against each other.

"Dad said I could have…"

"Mam said we're allowed…"

"Dad, you're ruining my life! I'm telling Mam."

And each one requires at least eighteen years of care and attention; that's 157,680 hours for those keeping score.

Life will present inevitable frustrations for everyone along the way. The store will run out of Lego. A friend will disappoint. A job won't work out. A relationship will end. You'll set out in one direction, and life will take you in another.

Some days, I'm up before the kids because I can get a little of something the house lacks during the day: silence. On other days, I meditate when they're at school, with friends or asleep. I've meditated alone and in company. I've meditated in office meeting rooms, fields, cars, trains, buses, saunas, hot tubs and once while locked in the toilet.

Some mornings, I sit in my home office chair and last all of thirty seconds before one of the kids barges in to see what's happening.

"Nothing is happening. That's the whole point!"

They never listen.

Meditation represents the inner stroke, a way of restoring equilibrium before stepping out into the day... or after retreating from it. Meditation helps a lot.

Unless it doesn't.

That's when consistency, presence and routine help. Sitting and focusing on your breath won't change a nappy, cook dinner, placate a temper tantrum or pay the mortgage. They represent the outer stroke, a way of guiding your family boat through in the world.

Still, every dad can learn how to inhale and exhale, even if they swear a little underneath.

The nineteenth-century American novelist William Dean Howells said, "Some people can stay longer in an hour than others can stay in a week."

Staying an hour in a small-town bookshop or in traffic

can feel like a week for a parent. Like that stressed-out mother, I still walk away when I'm losing it.

But I remember to come back eventually. That's the job. Until then...

Count backwards from ten.

Breathe, damn it.

Breathe.

Takeaways

Raising kids is a happy privilege, but it's also stressful. Don't let anyone tell you otherwise. Calmness is a skill worth developing for your sanity and also for setting a good example for your children.

Still, it's fine to lose patience with the kids occasionally. After all, they don't always trade in logic and reason.

If possible, avoid putting yourself in situations where you'll have to correct them in public for behaviours that are OK at home.

Many practices can help you cope with the inevitable stresses of family life. Meditation and journaling are two examples that worked for me. They're cheap and work almost anywhere. I usually meditate and journal in the mornings or evenings. Suffice to say, drinking and rumination do not. I save that for Saturday night.

Audrey enjoys preparing fancy cocktails, meeting her friends for dinner and long walks.

Other dads I know enjoy playing poker, watching football and fishing. You might even bond with your son or daughter over one of these hobbies when they're older. Until then, cultivate little respites for you and your partner. They offer a chance to recharge and approach family issues with a new lease of energy.

Mindful Tips

- Use apps like Headspace or Waking Up to learn the basics of meditation. They even offer short sessions for kids.
- If you're shopping with small kids, bring a "Break in Case of Emergencies" snack. It's amazing how much of a distraction food is.

TWENTY-NINE

MEMORIES

One winter, I'll be
Looking at French holiday snaps
With no kids by my side.

Family life presents many everyday moments worth remembering, even if we forget about the good times.

"You went to Disney World last year, Bryan?" said Audrey's aunt.

We were out for Sunday afternoon dinner in a local Italian restaurant with her family, Audrey, my mother-in-law and the kids.

"When our kids were small, we took them to Florida too," she said.

"It's a magical place," I said. "M-A-G-I-C-A-L."

"I don't remember much about that holiday," said her cousin. "It feels like a lifetime ago."

Audrey's uncle looked into his pint glass and swirled his beer. "That holiday costs us thousands. We saved for months."

I pictured his hours of overtime, the frugal weekends and months working towards one big holiday. And now... nothing more than an unreliable memory from years ago.

"She forgets it because she has so many wonderful memories from childhood," said my mother-in-law.

I wanted her to be right.

The year before, I'd saved up to fly the kids from Dublin to Florida. We spent two weeks in the heat, enjoying the rides in Disney World and Universal Studios.

The holiday cost as much as a small, troublesome car. Audrey prepared a timetable for each day, and we planned out all of the rides in advance. I wanted them to cherish every memory... especially the ones we paid so much to create.

After dinner, I grilled Sam about his cherishing.

"What was your favourite part of Disney World?" I said. "The Tower of Terror? Animal Kingdom? The fire-breathing dragons on Main Street? I want to know."

"I don't remember much of it," he said.

"Any of it?"

"I dunno, Dad, it was ages ago."

What is it with kids and their sense of time? What seems like yesterday to me is a lifetime for someone under ten. I want to give them a good childhood, and they don't have the decency to remember I tried!

"You know what I really want to know, Dad?" said Sam. "Where are we going next year?"

What Kids Forget

Next to day trading on the stock market, reading a book on an iPhone and the Atkins Diet, I consider trying to create perfect childhood memories as one of the most frustrating experiences in the world.

You can't control what your kids will remember or forget, and another family is probably having a better time, anyway. You want to do a good job as a dad, so you invest time, attention and even money into their upbringing, and then they go ahead and remember the shouting match over Sunday dinner years ago.

In 2018, we moved house from one end of the town to the other. Maria was eight at the time. Two years later, I asked her about the old townhouse where she'd spent *three-quarters of her life*.

"What can you remember? Your friends, your room, the colour I painted the kitchen?"

"Not much," she said.

"You must remember something! What about the Princess Anna *Frozen* doll you got for Christmas or the sleepover before your best friend moved to Canada?"

"I had a small bedroom, I prefer it here," said Maria.

Perhaps I expected too much, but I felt hard done by. We'd invested a lot of time, worry and equity into creating little childhood moments. And now they'd vanished!

Kids might be the most future-focused little monsters I know.

They're concerned with what they need today and why you're not getting it for them faster.

A cold drink from the fridge, something to eat even though dinner will be ready in five minutes, a playdate with a friend, a favourite film on television, a YouTube video and whatever their older brother or sister is having.

Ask them what they did yesterday, and they'll string out a few sentences. Ask them about what they did a week or month or year ago, and they're going to need some serious prompting and maybe even hypo-regression therapy.

Still, here's a working list of things you should expect your kids to forget.

That they promised to go to bed on time.

To flush the bathroom toilet after use.

When they promised to stop stretching their arms and legs out to the four corners of your car and into their brother or sister's face.

That they've already seen their favourite television show or film five times today alone.

To brush their teeth in the morning.

That they ate the same curry, you cooked in their aunt's house and enjoyed it.

When to change out of dirty clothes.

Not to put clean clothes in the wash.

The magical fairy doesn't arrive to clean up the kitchen after dinner.

Large chunks of their childhood that passed by without serious incident or drama.

Perhaps these types of memories are more for parents. Events from my past are like rocks I can't get rid of, whereas events from my present day are like grains of sands that fall through my hands unless I hold them in my mind.

I look backwards; they look ahead.

What Kids Remember

I've a clear childhood memory of sitting on a wooden red, blue and yellow swing one Sunday afternoon in my grandparents' house. My grandfather knew the one thing that would win the affection of my brother and me: free money.

He produced two silver pound coins and pressed them into our sweaty palms. When we went back inside, my brother cried.

"I can't, I can't find my pound coin," he said.

"Have you looked outside in the garden?" said my mother.

"I swallowed it!"

"Oh my God."

Cue a trip to the local hospital for an X-ray. The doctors told him to let the coin pass normally.

I recounted this story years later only for my mother to reveal the entire incident happened to me, not to my brother. I'd somehow transferred the experience onto him and blocked out whatever happened to the pound coin. Our memories are untrustworthy friends. A single event can punctuate an entire experience.

Still, let's give kids some credit. Here's a list of things they'll remember.

The last time you and your partner argued in front of them. Expect this gem to come up when they visit their grandparents' house.

That their older brother or sister can stay up an hour later.

Your promise from 337 days ago to host a sleepover.

Jammy doughnuts, chocolate ice cream and everything they're not supposed to eat too much of.

Their birthdays and Christmas.

Which parent is most likely to break under pressure and direct questioning first.

Don't Expect Any of This From Your Kids

Perhaps I'm being unfair. Memory is an unreliable friend for adults too. Think of it this way: as a dad, you probably remember explicit events and implicit ones. Explicit memory describes an event or occasion that's easy to recall. When your partner said, "I'm pregnant," for example. Childbirth. Their first few words. Starting school. That messy toilet training accident at the restaurant.

Not all of these explicit memories are particularly remarkable, either.

When I'm about to pop my clogs and the movie of my life flashes past my eyes, a good chunk will involve collecting my son or daughter from a friend's house: Sam or Maria looking for their shoes while I stand on the doorstep and asking another parent about the weather, work and where they're going on holiday.

I can explicitly remember saving for months to go to Disney World, flying across the Atlantic, queueing up for the Tower of Terror in Disney and agreeing with the kids over chicken wings that the queues were totally worth it.

Explicit memories aren't all good either. We're likely to remember negative experiences like a broken bone, a messy argument in front of the kids or even when a parent walked out. Those negative experiences punctate the good times.

Audrey's cousin and her younger brother, like our kids, didn't explicitly remember the trip to Disney World because it was one positive childhood experience lined up against another.

Perhaps it's too much to expect the kids to remember

family events in the same way as their parents. They can, however, draw on implicit memories.

Implicit memory describes an emotional recollection of a time or experience. You remember what going on holidays with your parents felt like, even if the location or specifics are vague – the excitement of packing your bags, getting onto a plane and the strange heat of a new country.

He Drank a Magic Potion

One Christmas Eve a few years ago, Sam couldn't sleep. He was too excited about all the presents that lay ahead. On a whim, Sam's uncle prepared a magic potion of hot chocolate and marshmallows. He fell asleep a few minutes after finishing the drink, and he insisted on a magic potion every year.

Sam is long past the point of believing in Santa Claus, but now all the kids insist on a hot chocolate with marsh-mallows when their uncle visits on Christmas Eve.

Family traditions serve as nice anchor points for families to hold on to. They're an odd combination of the explicit and implicit.

As a dad, you can also lay down the foundations of good childhood memories from little things like playing in the snow, taking them swimming or to the coffee shop for sticky buns. Think of these activities as deposits in their memory bank. They might not talk about them much today or tomorrow, but years later, they'll have something to look back upon.

When my son or daughter tell me they can't remember the specifics of an expensive holiday or what it was like to live in our old house, I remind myself that's OK.

It's a sign they've less baggage than adults to hold on to. Perhaps they can even teach me how to let go of my worries and focus on what's happening today.

Takeaways

Growing kids still won't remember every moment you spent with them, and you probably won't remember every second of parenting time either. They're more likely to remember something remarkable and out of the ordinary. That includes a firework display at the end of a big family holiday and also a shouting match over Sunday dinner from years ago.

Kids like to look ahead rather than backwards. "What's next?", "Are we there yet?" and "When can I have some?"

A combination of out the ordinary experiences, family traditions and little moments will give them something to draw on when they're older and worrying about going prematurely grey from the stress of raising their own small families.

Tips for Them Remember You By

- On the last day of a big family holiday, arrange something memorable or out of the ordinary, like a trip to see a firework display or extra desserts. In 2018, I interviewed Daniel Pink about his book, *When*[1]. He explained people are far more likely to remember ending an experience on a high.
- Taking photos, recording videos and journaling

are good ways of capturing what happened during the weekend or over the holidays. Thanks to cloud storage and apps like 1-Second Everyday, you can back up snaps from family holidays online and never lose them again.

THIRTY

CHOP WOOD, CARRY WATER

Chop wood, carry
Water, chop wood, carry water,
chop wood, carry water.

———————

Dads face many little jobs every day. Some are tedious, some are fun, and a few will last a lifetime.

Parenting, particularly small kids, is often an exercise in repetition and monotony.

I pick the same Lego blocks up off the floor every night, fight with the buckles of a car seat, change a conveyor belt of nappies, try to explain why plastic toys worth two cents and imported from China don't come with batteries, and slave on an assembly line of minor household chores all in the vain hope that they'll eat their broccoli, do their maths homework, grow up without taking drugs (at least in my house), forget the time I was too hungover to get up out of bed and cheer them on at their football match, and still love me when I'm eighty-eight, incontinent, staring into a nappy and wondering, *How did this happen to me?*

The great lie about parenting is we're supposed to treasure *every moment*. Kids grow up so fast, and parents experience something magical, each day better than the last.

Yes, they're growing so fast it'll catch your breath and *some moments* are worth treasuring.

But, how much should you value those mornings when your daughter, sixty seconds before an annual work review over Zoom, throws herself on the floor and screams, "I want Lilly to come over to play, it's so unfair. You're ruining my life." I can also recount four or five messy toilet-training episodes I'd rather not relive either.

How much should my mother value working all week and then waking up early one Saturday to find her two darling boys drinking baby paracetamol from the bottle?

How much should my parents value the Sunday when they went shopping for the afternoon and arrived home to find their oldest blind drunk on their vodka and passed out on the couch after vomiting in the back garden?

If I sound like a burnt-out dad, far from it.

One evening, after the kids were in bed, I came across an ancient Zen proverb about the meditative nature of everyday life: "Chop wood, carry water."

I don't spend much time chopping actual wood or even carrying water (unless plastic cups of juice to a toddler count), but I'm all about tree-related conundrums. The gist of this advice is beginners, experts and everyone in between face daily mundane tasks that demand their attention. These tasks, whether we like them or not, are character building.

So, instead of becoming overly analytical or emotional, focus on the everyday task at hand. When feeling confused about what to do next, take one step at a time, and the answers will reveal themselves.

Chopping wood and carrying water applies to parenting too.

Still, it's one thing to read about Zen on a quiet Sunday evening when the kids are asleep. It's quite another to put it into practice.

Smashing Lego Towers

Audrey bought K a large box of Lego blocks. After she opened the box, he clapped his hands and poured the blocks onto the floor.

He liked stacking dozens of the blocks on top of each other until they stood on the floor or kitchen table like the Leaning Tower of Pisa.

And then? He picked up his tower and threw it on the ground. *Smash!*

He was a master at building and smashing but less so at sorting and tidying.

Audrey (mostly) and I gathered the blocks from the kitchen floor and underneath the couch three or four times a day. It might have been more.

I stopped counting.

After we tidied the blocks away, K took the Lego back out of the toy box, built another tower and toppled it over.

We *could* have put the Lego box out of reach, but stacking the blocks on top of each other kept him busy and quiet.

Parents worry themselves unnecessarily with kids, particularly small ones.

Will they hurt themselves? Are they sick? Am I doing a good enough job?

Few moments are sweeter than when the ones you're responsible for are quiet, busy, and playing safely within eyesight.

But a man could go mad endlessly standing on, swearing at, picking up and tidying away the same set of Lego blocks day after day.

Not me.

I've picked up this mantra, you see: Chop wood, pick up Lego. Chop wood, pick up Lego. It's either that or lose it.

The Art of Archery

"I can't believe the zipline is closed," said Maria. "It's so unfair. It's the one thing I wanted to do here."

We were away for the bank holiday weekend at an Irish holiday camp set in a forest. Maria wanted to spend Saturday morning on the zipline, but a storm had damaged the ride a few days prior.

"How about archery instead?" said the instructor.

"I'm not sure about that. I wanted to use the zipline," said Maria.

"Let's go down, and you can have a look," I said.

We got on our bikes and cycled down to the range.

"Do you even know what archery is?" I said.

"Is it kind of like paintball?"

"I thought you were a clever clogs."

"I am!"

"You've a bit of work to do today. Lock your bike to the rack, and I'll explain."

At the range, the instructor, a local guy in his early twenties with a mop of blond hair and a flat Midlands accent, demonstrated how to use the bow and arrow.

"Will you stay?" whispered Maria.

"If they let me."

The instructor looked at his clipboard.

"Maria, you're up!"

I stood to accompany Maria into the firing range.

"I'm afraid no spectators are allowed inside," said the instructor. He pointed towards a bench in a wooden hut by the entrance.

"Wait over there, please."

"Remember, draw back the bow all the way. Use your muscles," I said to Maria. "Take the shot, and you won't go wrong."

She flexed her arms.

I walked back to the bench while Maria stepped onto the range. She tried to notch her first arrow, only to drop it on the ground.

"Pull the bow back some more," said the instructor. "All the way back."

Maria fired her second arrow into the ground. Her third arrow bounced off the wooden base, at the foot of the target: a plastic wolf.

After watching Maria shoot a few more rounds, I gave her a thumbs up and left her to it. I went for a short run around the campsite lake. I returned half an hour later to collect her.

"How is Maria getting on?" I asked the instructor.

"She's playing a stormer!"

"A stormer?"

I looked at Maria.

"I want to stay, Dad. Can I?"

"Sure."

Maria picked up her bow, notched an arrow, drew back and took the shot. I held my breath.

Twang

The arrow buried into the plastic wolf, an inch deep.

Sometimes, kids best carry their own water.

Listen Up! Zone Out

Dinnertime is one of the few moments in the day when everyone assembles from the four corners of our house.

One evening, Sam took a plate of food and sat down at the table, nodding his head while listening to music on his new pair of noise-cancelling headphones, freshly delivered by Jeff Bezos and his army of drones.

I called Sam's name a few times. I tried waving. I sent up smoke signals. Nothing. So I reached over and pulled the headphones down onto his shoulders.

"You can't even hear what we're saying," I said. "Take off those overpriced ear cans at the dinner table."

Sam swore a little. So I explained what constituted good table manners.

One of the great joys of parenting a teenager is getting into a long monologue in front of a captive yet reluctant audience.

"Alright, I get it, I get it," he said. "I'm trying to listen to music. You're always on my case."

He might be right.

That's one of my new jobs: getting on his case.

"Learning how to eat dinner and talking to the rest of us isn't something you can order from Amazon Prime," I said. "What album are you listening to, anyway?"

"An album? Who has time to listen to one artist for a whole hour?"

Sam, like any Generation Z teenager, can listen to all the music he wants or watch the latest shows almost immediately using Spotify and Netflix.

I explained how back in my day, I saved my pocket money for weeks, got the bus into the city centre to buy the album, and spent all weekend listening to *Definitely Maybe* by Oasis and the two other albums I owned on CD and tape.

"That sounds like a lot of work," he said.

"That's the point!"

But delayed gratification is a difficult concept for some adults to grasp, let alone teenagers.

"I'll WhatsApp you a few albums to listen to," I said.

"They're probably terrible."

"Can you take those headphones off your...?"

Chop wood, carry water. Chop wood, carry water.

The Work, It Never Ends

"Your house looks run down," said my mother.

She was right. Thankfully, we were moving out at the time.

Bent nails and old hooks stuck out from the chipped walls, ugly and exposed without pictures. The beige carpet was faded and frayed. The bathroom grout was chipped, and the wooden stair bannisters were scratched and marked.

I could barely hang a shelf without it falling off the walls, so I was glad to leave these undone tasks behind. When we moved into our new house, I was free from my never-ending to-do list of DIY chores.

Moving day offers a chance to see what a house is like without make-up.

Our old house could contain a family of three, but it bulged at the seams with five of us. The walls of our new house smelt of shiny, off-white paint. Everything glistened.

The bathrooms looked as if someone had unwrapped the cellophane and taken it out of a rather expensive box.

We brought the kids with us too.

In the attic, I stored a new cordless screwdriver next to a box of paints and paintbrushes, all unopened, unused and unloved – like a picture of Dorian Gray.

One day, one day.

It didn't take long for a toddling baby to bash into the kitchen and living room walls. His careening orange and green stroller took alarming chunks of wood out of the freshly-painted white skirting boards. Sam lucked out with an en suite bathroom and promptly informed his parents it wasn't his job to clean it. Maria's friends came to visit. They marched up and down the stairs, putting their hands and fingerprints all over the off-white walls.

"It's impossible to keep these walls clean when everyone runs their hands along them," I said to Audrey after they'd left for the night.

"You just hate DIY," said Audrey.

Damn right.

"We've only been in the house a few months," I said. "And it already looks old and battered. The new place will look like the old place in no time."

One wet Sunday afternoon, I took down the paintbrush, opened a can of paint and touched up the handprints. I filled in a few of the holes in the skirting boards too. I even charged the cordless screwdriver.

Our new house has more than enough space for the five of us, although that doesn't take away from the work of maintaining it.

Some scuff marks were OK.

Perhaps a showhouse should sparkle to capture the attention of would-be buyers. But a family home, rather than appearing like it's been unwrapped, finds character through its marks, dents and scratches; they say, "People live here."

Through these chinks and holes, that's how the light gets in.

Or perhaps it's, "Chop wood... take your hands off my walls because I've spent the past two bloody hours painting them!"

Zen is odd like that.

Takeaways

Dads perform the same tasks a lot: changing nappies, sterilising bottles, preparing or cleaning up after dinner, putting them to bed, getting them up, checking homework, prompting them to wash their teeth, go to bed, and so on.

These daily tasks are repetitive and constant, like chopping blocks of wood and carrying pails of water. You'll do them every day for a long time, and then one day you won't. Sometimes they'll feel hard and monotonous, but they're key to building up your character.

Becoming a dad is a process rather than an event. A guy acquires the necessary skills as much through everyday tasks as the Wednesday evening when you left work early to watch your son's team win a dramatic football final.

It's OK if some tasks are exhausting. Step back and consider if any of these daily tasks have a type of meditative quality you can sink into.

It could be something simple like washing the dishes after dinner or something more enjoyable like asking your son about school while driving him to football training.

It's helpful to say to yourself at the end of the day, "This could be the last time I feed him a bottle or read her a book."

I also like trying, "This is something we looked forward to, for a long time."

Hitting the target every now and then is nice, but taking the shot with your kids matters more.

Zen Tips

- Instead of feeling guilty when the kids say, "I'm bored," let them revel in it. Or, as George Carlin once said about entertaining bored kids, "Go out and dig a hole."[1] Learning how to fill free hours independently and spending time alone is a big part of life.
- Encourage your older kids to help out with simple chores like taking out the bins, cleaning up after dinner, and even bringing the dog for a short walk. Chopping wood and carrying water applies to them too!

THIRTY-ONE

THE SNIP

Incision, don't look
Pulling, tugging, snip, snip
No babies? Hurrah!

––––––––––

Many dads have illogical fears about vasectomies, but they're a reliable, common and painless form of contraception.

Several months before K was born, I announced to my wife, "I want to get a vasectomy, and I want to do it next week."

"I've heard this before," she said, rolling her eyes. "I'll believe it when it happens."

"It's already happened!" I said, pointing to her bump.

"If I don't get a vasectomy soon, another one will arrive, I know it. I'm done, spent, worn out."

"I can't get pregnant again when I'm like this."

We planned baby number three and agreed three kids were enough, for us at least.

Some friends have four kids, and my wife comes from a large family. But three is a nice round number.

Nature wants to breed. It's indifferent to whether a stressed Irish dad has one kid or half a dozen.

I was always suspicious of contraception. Years ago, I found out the pill has a 91% success rate.

Played out over a lifetime, the numbers weren't in my favour and that's before considering forgetfulness or an illness flushing contraception from the body.

We've tried other types of contraception over the years, and I'm sure they work well for other couples. But I liked the finality of a vasectomy. If I'm honest, it's something I can control. And unlike a condom, it's unlikely to break.

"But, can you at least wait until after the baby arrives safely?" Audrey said.

She wasn't due to give birth for a few months.

I usually research and over-analyse every small and big decision. If the Olympics gave out medals for rumination, I'd win gold.

While waiting until D-Day, I read up and asked around about the pros and cons of vasectomies.

Oddly enough, I worried one would affect my drive: that I'd lie in bed late every morning eating cheesy Doritos and watching Netflix instead of getting up for work or the gym.

Some men also worry getting one will affect their testosterone count, that they won't be able to enjoy any of their old interests or even ejaculate.

When I told a friend about my plans, he said, "I'd worry I'd lose my drive closing deals at work. I'd let people take advantage of me."

"The kids take advantage of me all the time!" I said.

The moral argument for vasectomies intrigued me. It was useful fodder for pub debates. If I bought into the concept of overpopulation, getting one represents doing my bit to save the planet from overpopulation.

Alas, my intentions weren't so noble. I wanted to avoid worrying about an unplanned pregnancy or changing nappies and pushing buggies in my mid-sixties. Parenting, in my world, is a young man's game.

While medical advice helped, I wanted to hear real-world stories from people who'd faced the snip and survived. I cornered Michael, an old friend with four kids.

He took little convincing to regale me with his vasectomy-gone-wrong story.

"I'll never forget the pain of recovery," he said. "I was limping for weeks."

He grabbed his crotch for emphasis.

"I'm pretty sure that's not supposed to happen," I said. "Did you get a receipt?"

Other people's reactions were surprising.

"Aren't you a little young for getting a vasectomy," said one friend.

"We started early!"

"But what if you meet someone who wants kids later on?"

She changed the subject quickly. The subtext being: *what if you get a divorce and your next partner wants kids?*

Meeting the needs of some future partner lay far beyond my imagination.

K was born in September. I arranged my appointment for October. During the pre-consult, the doctor walked me through a series of questions.

"Have you talked the procedure and its implications over with your partner?"

"Yes. She's just had a baby. She says she's done too."

"Do you know this procedure is difficult to reverse?"

"Wanting a reversal won't be a problem. He's number three. I'm fifteen years in."

"And do you know how a vasectomy works?"

"I've got this friend who walked me through it..."

The doctor took out a plastic model of the penis and explained how he was going to cut my vas deferens.

The testicle manufactures sperm and testosterone, but it transports the latter through your bloodstream and not to the vas deferens (aka the carrying-away vessel that transports sperm before ejaculation).

Seeing a sense of confusion and anxiety creep across my face, he answered the one question every man has about a vasectomy: does an ejaculation feel the same after the snip?

"You won't notice a difference. Everything works as a normal," he said. "The river flows, but your swimmers are out of the race."

When he put the model away, I told the doctor about my friend's botched procedure.

"Are they foolproof doc?" I said. "Give it to me straight."

"Nothing is foolproof," he said. "But the odds of one not taking are less than a thousand."

I could live with those odds.

So, I booked in for the procedure on a Saturday afternoon one week before my thirty-seventh birthday: an early present to myself.

Doing My Bit

The doctor brought me into a small treatment room at the back of the medical clinic, and he introduced me to the nurse. I felt like I was at a big end-of-year exam I'd forgotten to study for.

"Rita will assist with the procedure," he said. "She's my wife."

"Relax," she said. "We've completed hundreds of these procedures."

I wondered if this husband and wife vasectomy team talked about work much at home over dinner?

Hey honey, this guy came into the office today with some crazy theories about the vas deferens and doing his bit for overpopulation.

She gave me a gown to change into. I placed my feet on stir-ups either side of the bed, opened my legs and hoisted the gown up.

The doctor got to work. I felt a short, sharp pain when he injected a numbing agent around the side of each testicle.

After that, a numbness spread between my legs, kind of like the sensation before getting a filling extracted, except lower down.

I didn't look. It's one thing to know you're getting a vasectomy, but it's quite another to see someone going at you with scissors or a scalpel. I stared hard at a sunlight window on the ceiling instead.

After a few minutes, the doctor began tugging and pulling, but the procedure felt as if it were happening to someone else.

I'm good at compartmentalising. Still, my head invents

problems where there aren't any: *What if the doctor cut the wrong wire?*.

"How long have you been running the practice for?"

"Almost thirty years."

"Wow, did you ever think of retiring?"

"Actually, I'm thinking about it next year, but I haven't decided what to do with all my patients yet."

"Would another doctor take them up?"

"They might."

Nothing like a little business talk between a doctor and his patient.

He picked up a blade. The steel gleamed in afternoon sun pouring in via a skylight.

"What's the typical age range of somebody who gets a vasectomy?" I said.

"Oh, between your age and about fifty."

"Do they usually have kids?"

"Almost always."

I was joining an exclusive club!

Around the ten-minute mark, I heard a distinct *snip*. And the doctor moved to my other side.

A few minutes later... *snip*.

A little later, the doctor put his tools back in the tray and wheeled his chair away.

"We're done," he said, "You can get dressed now. You'll be pleased to know there wasn't any blood."

I washed up and got dressed. I couldn't tell if the warm sensation in my stomach was relief or the affect-effects of the numbing agent.

"It will take at least thirty ejaculations to take complete effect," he said in his office afterwards.

Like cleaning the pipes.

"You also need to get a specimen tested before having unprotected sex."

I shook the doctor's hand.

"You walked me through the procedure nicely," I said.

The doctor looked like I was thanking him for fixing the car, but what did other men say afterwards?

I spent the rest of the day sitting on the couch watching a *Star Wars* film, as per doctor's orders to avoid anything strenuous for twenty-four hours.

After the kids's bedtimes, I peeled off the bandages and inspected myself in the mirror. Apart from some faint yellow bruising and two minor nicks from this doctor's incisions, everything looked normal.

Everything felt normal.

Results

Once the nicks closed up, I couldn't spot a difference between life before and after.

Over the next few weeks, I didn't lose the will to live, and I still wanted to run, lift weights, work on my business and generally get on with the things.

The procedure appeared successful, but gut intuition is hardly a reliable form of contraception.

I needed to get a test or specimen analysis at the local hospital to confirm the procedure worked.

I was embarrassed about the idea of ejaculating into a cup and producing it to a nurse. Could I really perform under such pressure?

I put off getting a specimen analysis for a few weeks and then a few months. The more time passed, the easier it was to forget all about the test.

A year and a half went by.

One evening, I met Michael for a beer. I told him about the vasectomy and my recovery.

"What about you?"

"After all that, the vasectomy didn't take," he said. "My tubes re-knitted themselves. I'm the most fertile man in Ireland."

His wife nodded in confirmation, while their four kids ran around the kitchen.

"He's getting another one."

The whole thing was like a family lore, one for the grandkids.

I booked in for a specimen analysis the following day. A month later, I performed under pressure and brought a medically-sealed container ensconced in a brown envelope to the local hospital. Even while parking the car outside, I looked around, hoping I wouldn't see anyone I knew.

In the treatment room, the nurse asked me to complete a form.

"You forgot one section."

I looked at the paperwork:

Semen produced on:

Number of days of abstinence:

She helpfully pointed to the last section.

Time of ejaculation (from sexual intercourse/masturbation to semen collection):

What was the average? Did people come in and surprise the clinic with figures like twenty two minutes?

A month later, the five of us went away for the bank holiday weekend to Rosslare. It's a sleepy village on the coast in Co.Wexford.

We didn't do much.

The highlight of the day involved watching K. run up a

moderately sized hill with Maria and then running back down without falling over.

Afterwards, went out for dinner to a fancy seafood restaurant for an early bird. In between the mussels and steak, my phone rang.

"Hello Bryan."

I instantly recognised the doctor's voice, smooth like melting butter. I excused myself from the table and stepped out into the street

"The results of your specimen analysis came back the other day and I've some good news, it's all clear."

"So the procedure worked?"

"Yes, there was nothing present. Was this your first time going for an analysis test?"

Pause.

"I put it off, Doc."

He laughed.

"Well, thanks again."

"You're very welcome."

I sat down at the table and leaned against my chair. My oldest son was sawing into a fillet steak of his own, my daughter dipping the last of her chips into hot gravy, and the baby was already on to his ice-cream, chocolate sauce dribbling down his chubby chin.

"Would sir like anything else?" said the server.

"You know what," I said, leaning back into my chair. "I'm about done."

Takeaways

Getting a vasectomy isn't a small decision. If you're thinking of one, talk through the consequences with your partner. Are you both happy that your family is complete?

I'd also recommend avoid making a decision about a vasectomy in the immediate aftermath of an unplanned pregnancy or a new arrival.

It's best to live with the idea of having no more kids for a few months before taking action. Prior to the procedure, it's normal to feel nervous. Once it's over sex and life will return to normal quickly. You also won't have to worry about any more unexpected events. It's a liberating experience for dads.

Snippety, Snip Tips

- Take the day off work for the snip, but that's probably enough. Recovery is quick and easy. The doctor cleared me for a run two days later.
- Don't make my mistake. Book in for the follow-up as soon as you can after the procedure. As the days go by, it gets easier to put something off.

MASTERY

Five of us, around a table, eating pizza.
It's later than we think.

Obviously, I'm not done.

It's a fine image, Audrey, Sam, Maria and K in a fancy restaurant on a long bank holiday weekend. Bills paid, job security, plans for tomorrow and closure around what our family looks like.

I'm sipping beer, watching Audrey wipe pasta sauce off the baby's chubby chin while Sam and Maria are getting on during the brief respite between steaks and chocolate dessert.

It's also a snapshot of a moment in time.

Uncle Ben told Peter Parker, "With great power comes great responsibility."

He might as well have been talking about raising a child.

Parenting is a long, ambling march with no real finish line. And I'm only one teenager in with another two following close behind. I'll be over fifty and bald by the time Sam is rich, Maria organising my late-mid-life crisis and K grown up and grumbling about kids of his own.

Even then, I'll attempt to dispense some advice and set some new boundaries.

"When I was in my twenties, I tried that. And I tried that too. It didn't work. Trust me, don't even think about it. What you need to do is run more, and meditate, and lift weights. Keep going, keep going."

Sometimes, I enjoy telling older parents of grown-up kids that I'm nearly done. (If they push me on it, I explain the snip.)

"The oldest, he's eighteen in a few short years. I'll see you guys at the responsibility-free club soon! I'm going to stay out all night. No one can stop me."

These grey-haired parents and grandparents take particular delight in saying, "You never give up being a parent or stop worrying about them."

They could be right, but it's hard to take them too seriously because they're usually on the way to the pub or getting ready for their third or fourth fancy holiday of the year on a cruise ship or in the south of France.

Would I do it all over again?

The late nights (sitting in, that is) and early mornings. The division of labour. The negotiations with a partner finding her own way as a mother. The worries about money and job security. The painful hard mistakes and lessons learnt, over and over. The shifting tide of friendship between those with and without kids. The endless questions and me with no answers. The awesome weight of holding a newborn baby you'll raise, the measure of a lifetime.

Absolutely.

I'd still like to go back and change my approaches and several decisions, particularly back in the early days. Writing this book, I'm struck by how clueless I was and how much of my baggage and expectations I brought to the dad role.

A therapist told me, "We're defined by the experiences we have in childhood. They can take a lifetime to understand."

We got around to working on some of that baggage from childhood. I even turned some of those sessions into stories for this book.

I wrote this chapter a few months before my fortieth birthday, an occasion that marks the end of youth. I'm an adult on paper, but I'm still trying to unpick all those subtle childhood moments that rise up at odd times, like at two-twenty-three on a dreary grey Tuesday afternoon in between work conference calls.

I'm willingly or otherwise creating moments for my three kids to either appreciate, learn from or solve when they're older.

I'd change a few other things, like meditating more and worrying less about what a dad should and shouldn't do, but not much.

I'm conscious that if I pull too much on a particular string, the entire tapestry will fall apart in my hands. Despite the subtle imperfections, it's a gift to behold.

Malcolm Gladwell[1] popularised the idea of the Ten Thousand Hour Rule: it takes approximately ten years of practice to develop mastery in a craft, a statistic I'm prone to citing a lot. Over the years, I've tried tracking hours spent on personal pursuits like writing and running, so I could gauge my progress. I haven't tracked how many hours I've put in with the three kids. But I know this much. I'm over fifteen years in. Surely that's more than the prescribed 10,000 hours?

Will I get a sticker, medal or another participation award from the other dads in the pub, at the gym or in the local athletics club? Does any of it transform me into a master at the delicate art of parenting?

No.

At best, I know a lot about my kids, as any dad should about their kids.

In fact, if you come around these parts with a crying baby or a teenager in trouble, I'll commiserate and then wish the two of you on your merry way. I'll even ring the taxi.

I've my own problems to deal with.

Only a parent can unlock the unique puzzle of their offspring. The doctors, therapists, parenting experts, aunts, uncles, cousins and even the grandparents... they're all kind of like big-hearted financial advisors that come with a disclaimer.

Past performance doesn't guarantee future returns. Take from them what works. Chuck away the rest with the baby clothes destroyed during toilet training.

That said, I can't resist.

If I've learnt one thing about parenting since Audrey announced "I'm pregnant" back in 2006 when I was fresh-faced, slick with hair gel and wrinkle-free, it's this:

Every regular guy needs to find their own way with the little people in their lives. Sometimes they agree on a direction with a partner. Perhaps they walk the same road? One leads for a while, and one follows.

Different choices are OK.

Occasionally, a guy wanders down the wrong path for weeks, months or years (*hopefully not*) before asking someone for directions and hurrying back on track with the little people in his life.

He scouts ahead, calling "Keep up," and replies for the dozenth time, "No, we're not there yet." He picks his daughter up when she falls, and he shows his son the way.

They walk the road together, and one day, a dad looks his son or daughter in the eye, and neither can believe how far they've come.

ABOUT THE AUTHOR

Bryan Collins lives an hour outside Dublin in Ireland with his wife and three kids.

When he's not debating the merits of giving the kids snacks after dinner, he's huffing and puffing in the local park, trying to lift heavy things or procrastinating on his phone.

He runs a popular website and podcast for new writers at https://becomeawritertoday.com

You can also read more of Bryan's work for free by joining his newsletter at http://bryancollins.com

 twitter.com/bryanjcollins

RESOURCES FOR DADS

Whether you are a seasoned dad or are expecting your first child, books are invaluable resource for today's dads. These books cover the full gamut from what to expect to how to handle difficult temper tantrums. The best ones are also honest about what parenting is really like.

1. *The Gardener and the Carpenter* by Alison Gopnik

Clinical psychologist and philosopher Alison Gopnik challenges the 21st-century view of parenting in this book. This book is a great gift for new dads because it helps them learn to give themselves permission to have unpredictable and messy children.

2. *Talk so Kids Will Listen & Listen so Kids Will Talk* by Adele Faber and Elaine Mazlish

This book explores how to communicate with children in such a way that they will not only listen to the parent, but also want to talk to the parent. This team of New York Times bestselling authors teaches parents what to do with big feelings, both in themselves and in their kids, so that communication continues.

3. *Peaceful Parent, Happy Kids* by Dr Laura Markham

In Peaceful Parent, Happy Kids, Dr Laura Markham explores her clinical experience and the most current research on brain development to teach parents how to develop emotional connections with their children. Her belief is that having that connection means parents no longer have to yell, threaten or punish.

4. *The Whole-Brain Child* by Daniel J. Siegel, MD and Tina Bryson, Ph.D.

In The Whole-Brain Child, the authors explore neuroscience behind the developing mind and what it needs to grow into a healthy child. While it's a scientific approach to understanding the child's brain, it is written in a way that appeals to the everyday dad.

5. *Mayo Clinic Guide to Your Baby's First Year*

In this book, a team of pediatricians and baby experts explore development during the first year of a baby's life. When a new parent has a question in the middle of the night, this is the resource they can grab off the bookshelf to consult. It even includes growth charts to put worried parents' minds at ease.

6. *The Happiest Baby on the Block* by Harvey Karp

Every parent wants to have the happiest baby on the block, and Dr Harvey Karp wants to teach them how. This book focuses on sleep training and crying calming babies.

In this book, Dr Karp doesn't advocate sleep training through crying it out. He encourages parents to swaddle, shush and swing their babies, then use sucking reflexes and side positions to trigger the baby's natural calming abilities.

7. *The Emotional Life of the Toddler* by Alicia F. Lieberman

In The Emotional Life of the Toddler, Dr Lieberman explores why toddlers have explosive emotions. She teaches parents how to deal with tantrums and crying toddlers, what to do about screen time and how to ensure good development during this wild stage of life. It gives parents permission not to give in to every whim of their children's emotions.

8. *Dear Dory* by Tom Kreffer

I interviewed British author Tom Kreffer. He's the author of Dear Dory: Journal of a Soon to Be First Time Dad, which he initially wrote as a series of journal entries when his partner was expecting their first child, before turning it into a book. It's a good insight into the life of a modern expectant dad.

10. *The Erma Bombeck Collection: If Life Is a Bowl of Cherries, What Am I Doing in the Pits?, Motherhood, and The Grass Is Always Greener Over the Septic Tank* by Erma Bombeck

Erma Bombeck was an American humorist who wrote about family life and parenting in the 1970s, 1980s and early 1990s. Her audience was primarily women and mothers, although her colorful insights into family life apply today.

11. *Man vs. Child: One Dad's Guide to the Weirdness of Parenting* by Harry N. Abrams

This book is unlike the usual scientific-based parenting books. Instead, it's a colorful advice-driven book about how to get ready for your firstborn.

11. *The Expectant Father: The Ultimate Guide for Dads-to-Be* by Armin A. Brott

New York Times best-selling author Brott has written a series of popular books for new dads. His New Father series covers everything from pregnancy to navigating those first few years. This guide is the first step on your journey.

12. *Dad's Maybe Book* by Tim O'Brien

Tim O'Brien is well-known for his reportage of the Vietnam War and his literary novels. He also became a father late in life. In this book, which he wrote over the course of their childhood, O'Brien reflects on what it means to become a dad and on life lessons for his growing kids.

1 3. *Bare Minimum Parenting: The Ultimate Guide to Not Quite Ruining Your Child* by James Breakwell

Jame Breakwell is a master at turning family life into jokes and colorful stories. Check out his handle @explodingunicorn on Twitter for daily dad jokes. I also interviewed him for the Become a Writer Today podcast.

1 4. *We're Parents: The New Dad's Survival Guide to Baby's First Year* by Adrian Kulp

The first year with your first born is one of the hardest years any new parent will face. If you're looking for a survival guide, check this title out.

I also recommend checking out the excellent blog for dads, Fatherly.com

REMEMBER YOUR BONUS

If you'd like a free book from Bryan or would like to read more of his work, join his newsletter at bryancollins.com and claim a free book.

THE POWER OF CREATIVITY SERIES

The Power of Creativity

Learning How to Build Lasting Habits, Face Your Fears and Change Your Life

(Book 1)

An Uncommon Guide to Mastering Your Inner Genius and Finding New Ideas That Matter

(Book 2)

How to Conquer Procrastination, Finish Your Work and Find Success

(Book 3)

http://thepowerofcreativitybook.com

BECOME A WRITER TODAY SERIES

Yes, You Can Write!

101 Proven Writing Prompts that Will Help You Find Creative Ideas Faster for Your Journal, Blogging, Writing Your Book and More

(Book 1)

The Savvy Writer's Guide to Productivity

How to Work Less, Finish Writing Your Story or Book, and Find the Success You Deserve

(Book 2)

The Art of Writing a Non-Fiction Book

An Easy Guide to Researching, Creating, Editing, and Self-publishing Your First Book

(Book 3)

http://becomeawritertodaybook.com

ACKNOWLEDGEMENTS

I don't usually write about parenting. The inspiration from this book came from two separate conversations with Leah Komaiko and Bronagh, both of whom helped spark the idea in the first place. Thanks also to Sandy Draper for editing this book and Geoffrey Bunting for designing the cover.

REFERENCES AND FOOTNOTES

1. D-Day

1. Grossman, Martin. Engrossment. The Newborn's Impact on the Father. Obstetrical & Gynecological Survey. 1975. Accessed at https://journals.lww.com/obgynsurvey/citation/1975/02000/engrossment__the_newborn_s_impact_upon_the_father.5.aspx on May 19, 2021.

3. Guilty

1. In Ireland, kids commonly say Mam or Mammy in place of Mum or Mummy.
2. A bottle of milk.
3. The Irish equivalent of an airing cupboard.
4. Eisenberg, Arlene. *What to Expect When You're Expecting*. Simon & Schuster. 1984.
5. He has two kids now. When I ring him, he talks at great length about how busy they are. I laugh.
6. The local baby gym.
7. A soother, pacifier or dummy.

5. Sick

1. Thankfully, he's much happier these days living in a house semi-independently in the community.

7. The Gap

1. Accessed at https://www.latimes.com/sports/la-xpm-2014-apr-14-la-sp-sn-michael-phelps-swimming-20140414-story.html on June 16, 2021.
2. Gladwell, Malcolm. *Outliers: The story of Success*. Penguin. 2008.

10. Escape Valve

1. A prolific man in more ways that one, now he has four kids.
2. A small, sun-baked island off the south coast of Greece.

11. The Provider

1. Ireland's national broadcaster

12. Girls and Boys

1. . ... except when they aren't.
   Labelling sexes exclusively as male or female is binary and doesn't account for experiences of transgender, gender fluid and non-binary people.
   What I'm writing here is reflective of my experiences as a parent of two male boys and a female girl.
   Before sending in a letter of complaint, I couldn't write honestly about the experiences of parenting kids of other genders. It's not something I've experienced in my immediate family.
2. Biddulph, Steve. *Raising Boys in the 21st Century*. Harper Thorsons. 2013.
3. Irish slang for toilet
4. An Irish stick and ball game played by women, kind of like hurling.

13. Friends with Kids

1. Insert your knockoff alcohol brand of choice here.
2. British slang misappropriated by the Irish to describe feeling exhausted.
3. Irish slang describing somebody who's cheeky or talks back a lot to authority figures i.e. dads

14. Big Words

1. Orwell, George. *1984*. Penguin Essentials. 2021.

16. Discipline

1. An Irish colloquialism meaning "you're growing up"
2. He now has kids.

17. Bullies

1. The Irish version of high school.
2. One who observes their growing son or daughter's every movement and swoops in to intervene at the slightest sign of trouble.

18. Dad Science

1. Eisenberg, Arlene. *What to Expect When You're Expecting*. Simon & Schuster. 1984.

19. Keeping Score

1. Irish for boy.

21. Hair

1. A Ronnie is British and Irish slang for the overly-optimistic hints of a moustache.

24. Money

1. Pope, C. (15 August, 2016). "You want two children? That'll be €500,000 please", Irish Times. Accessed at https://www.irishtimes.com/news/consumer/you-want-two-children-that-ll-be-500-000-please-1.2754454 on February 9, 2021.

25. Best Friends

1. A popular Irish youth club with a strict no alcohol policy.
2. Irish and english slang for getting drunk.
3. Irish slang for drunk.
4. Slang for a personal argument or point of view.

26. The Plan

1. Rippetoe, Mark. *Starting Strength*. The Aasgaard Company. Kindle Edition. 2013.
2. His bathroom.

27. Promises, Promises

1. An Irish noun for flattery.
2. Oshiya (押し屋.

28. Breathe

1. Santideva (Author), Vesna A. Wallace (Translator), B. Alan Wallace (Translator). *A Guide to the Bodhisattva Way of Life*. Snow Lion. 1997.

29. Memories

1. Pink, D. When: *The Scientific Secrets of Perfect Timing* (p. 88). Canongate Books. Kindle Edition. 2018.

30. Chop Wood, Carry Water

1. Carlin, George. *It's Bad for Ya!* Laugh.com. 2016.

Mastery

1. Gladwell, Malcolm. *Outliers*. Little, Brown & Company. 2008.

Made in the USA
Columbia, SC
01 December 2021

50150212R00198